THE LIVING THOUGHTS LIBRARY
Edited by Alfred O. Mendel

MACHIAVELLI

THE LIVING THOUGHTS LIBRARY

Life travels upward in spirals. He who
takes pains to search the shadows of the past
below us, then, can better judge the tiny arc
up which he climbs, more surely guess the
dim curves of the future above him.

MACHIAVELLI

THE LIVING THOUGHTS OF

MACHIAVELLI

PRESENTED BY

COUNT CARLO SFORZA

CASSELL
AND COMPANY, LIMITED
LONDON, TORONTO, MELBOURNE
AND SYDNEY

Niccolò Machiavelli was born at Florence, on May 3, 1469. His father followed the profession of a jurist. In 1494 Niccolò, whose works show wide reading in the Latin and Italian classics, entered public life, serving Florence in many positions and various ways but in the end receiving only ingratitude. He was an inveterate opponent of the Medici tyrants, and in 1513 was imprisoned on a charge of conspiring against them. He was of middle height, black-haired, with a rather small head, very bright eyes and slightly aquiline nose. When he died on June 20, 1527, a poor man, nobody but himself thought that his works would last. They are *The Prince, The Florentine History, The Art of War*, Essays on Livy and government, and a couple of plays.

Translation of the Introductory Essay by Doris E. Troutman
Translation of the Private Letters by Dr. Arthur Livingston
The woodcut portrait of Machiavelli was made by
Professor Hans A. Mueller

First Edition . . . *November 1942*
Second Edition . . . *December 1945*

PRINTED IN GREAT BRITAIN BY
MORRISON AND GIBB LTD., LONDON AND EDINBURGH
1245

PRESENTING

MACHIAVELLI .

ANYONE WHO PLANS TO WRITE WITHOUT BIAS ABOUT Machiavelli will soon discover how difficult it is to find readers whose feelings and ideas have not been poisoned by some blind prejudice toward the Florentine secretary and his work. Almost unconsciously they still link the political thoughts of Machiavelli with the most objectionable political and moral controversies and theories of our time. Interestingly enough, this demonstrates to what extent Machiavelli is still alive.

The hatred unleashed against Machiavelli has been and still is moral, or pseudo-moral ; even worse, it stems from religious issues. And there is nothing more fierce among men (above all, among those who profess, or believe they profess, " Christian love ") than religious quarrels and fights.

Oddly enough, both the Roman Catholic and the Protestant Churches are in accord in their rabid condemnation of Machiavelli and the attempt to annihilate him. Yet, while their motive and the technique they employ are identical, each interprets the Florentine from opposing viewpoints. The Jesuits and other Catholic polemists of the Reformation's counter-reaction abominated in particular the Italian patriot in the Florentine secretary who—contrary to almost all the great Italians of his age—denounced the papacy's territorial ambitions and exposed them as one of the chief obstacles to national independence. Protestant writers, interpreting the same manuscript, sought to reveal Machiavelli as the personification of popish perfidy. That both succeeded in a measure becomes credible when we recall that *Jesuitism* in the eighteenth century stood for what formerly had been christened *Machiavellism*.

Machiavelli was the first great modern thinker. But in order for us to understand what that means it is not enough merely to study his works, his immortal discourses—*Discorsi sopra la prima Deca di Tito Livio*—which the prevailing fad for *The*

Prince has kept in the background for so many readers. We must first of all attempt to understand the medieval world out of which Machiavelli came, and why he was the first to realize that the institutions of that world no longer contained even the germ of productive life.

Francesco de Sanctis, the Italian literary critic and one of the most penetrating minds of the whole nineteenth century, begins his essay on Machiavelli by reminding us that the author of the *Discourses* had been present in Rome at the time *Orlando Furioso* was published, and that he complained about having been excluded—perhaps deliberately—from the large list of Italian poets recorded by Ariosto in the last *canto* of his poem. There could be nothing more human than Machiavelli, the most powerful political thinker of his time—perhaps of all time—wishing to be known for his poetry rather than for his political works.

This incident, a purely literary one, was evoked by de Sanctis to remind us that Machiavelli was born about the same time as the greatest poet of his era : Machiavelli in 1469, Ariosto in 1474—which was also the year of Michelangelo's birth. But Ariosto bears no resemblance to Machiavelli. *Orlando Furioso* was only the means through which the author was able to inject life into phantoms ; neither religion nor country made any claims on Ariosto, who was concerned only with perfection of form and with poetical inspiration. Ariosto was neither religious nor irreligious ; he was above all that. He believed only in Art. The world of the beginning of the sixteenth century was to him only a vast storehouse which could serve his poetical imagination, as did the Orlandos, the Rinaldos, the Angelicas and the Brandimartes, whom he merely lifted from the old period of chivalry, without even making them ridiculous, as Cervantes was to do much later.

To place Machiavelli in his time, to understand his inner revolts, and by what a truly heroic effort he completely liberated his spirit, we must recall that in 1497, at the age of twenty-eight, Machiavelli closely followed the passionate preachings (in the Florentine churches of Santa Reparata and San Marco) of Fra Girolamo Savonarola, the puritan monk who was the tyrannical moralist of Florence at that time, as Calvin was at Geneva during his lifetime—as well as after it. The passionate moralizings of Savonarola evidently left the young Florentine cold, because at the very moment when popular enthusiasm over the monk was growing more ecstatic Machiavelli wrote to a friend [1] with cold but extreme sarcasm : " He divides all men into two groups : the ones made for God — himself and his followers—and the others, headed for the Devil, who are his opponents."

What then did Savonarola really represent in that Florentine *fin de siècle*, where the spirit of Machiavelli was taking shape ?

Savonarola, like Christopher Columbus, was cut from the stuff out of which all heroes, martyrs and great thinkers are made. Columbus was navigating towards " India " when Savonarola appealed from the heights of his pulpit for a purified Christian society. The visions of both Italians were towards a new world, the extent or shape of which was unknown. Savonarola saw the misfortunes which were hurtling down on Italy ; he had foreseen the invasion of Charles VIII and his Frenchmen, and he imputed it to the only reasons by which a fanatical monk could explain it—the sins of mankind, the corrupt life of cities, the vengeance of God. Savonarola, an heroic figure, who would have fascinated Dante two centuries earlier, was the last luminous ray of lightning in the vanishing world of the Middle Ages. If Machiavelli was excessively bitter towards the terrifying, pure Dominican friar who made Pope and princes tremble, it was not out of indifference or because of scepticism. With his superb insight Machiavelli clearly saw what mistakes had been made, and precisely what interests were behind the invasion of Italy by foreign armies. Later, while studying the causes which had opened the way for the first invasion of Italy by France, with Savonarola in mind he wrote : " There is the reason why Charles of France could take possession of Italy, choosing his route with ease ; he who said that our sins were to blame spoke the truth, only, not the crimes he had in mind, but those which I described, were the cause."

Savonarola, who remained faithful to the most orthodox Catholicism up to the strangling gibbet, fervently strove to

[1] The letter, dated March 9, 1497, addressed to Ricciardo Bechi, is reproduced in this volume (pages 79–82).

bring about a vast reform of the clergy and popes; there is no doubt now that the territorial ambitions of the Church filled his pure soul with horror; Dante—sublimest of Catholic poets—felt the same disgust at the temporal power of the Pope. But read one of Machiavelli's passages on the popes as sovereigns of towns and provinces: "They are the only ones who have a state and do not defend it, who have subjects and do not govern them. As their states are not defended, no one feels tempted to conquer them; and as their subjects are not governed, they feel at ease and do not care to be delivered. Therefore, these states are secure and happy. But as they are administered by the powers above, on which the human spirit dares not touch, I do not want to speak of them; inasmuch as they are states maintained and protected by the Lord himself it would be presumptuous and reckless on my part to speak further of them." Compared with this cold irony the epigrams and caprioles of M. de Voltaire seem tame.

Although by the end of the fifteenth century it was known that only the application of the most drastic remedies could save Italy, minds such as Savonarola still thought it necessary to strengthen the institutions which had existed from the distant dawn of the Middle Ages. Only Machiavelli clearly understood the reality; only he comprehended that these solemn formulas, while still surrounded with universal veneration, were in reality nothing but sinister trappings from which all life had gone. Almost all the Italian people believed in the Church as the only political power; to them the city-state was a small beloved fatherland which bowed to the idea of the Empire as a symbol of the heirdom of Rome and the unity of Christian society. The Italian people wasted their time in talking and in longing for reforms; Machiavelli alone understood that it was necessary to rebuild from the ground up. As the first modern Italian who rejected all outmoded form, he understood that the Church and Empire were no longer living, political forces. Before him, if one was not Guelf, for the Pope, one was Ghibelline, for the Emperor. He — and only he — knew that the Guelfs and the Ghibellines were both dead.

Concerning the Church—the Church headed by Pope Alexander VI—he wrote: "In order to explain its decline one is compelled to state that the people who have least religion are the ones who are closest to the Church of Rome, the centre of our religion." About the Empire, and Caesar—the most celebrated hero of imperial legend, the hero worshipped by the Ghibellines of the Middle Ages as well as by the naïve Fascists of the twentieth century—he wrote : " Do not be mistaken about the so-called glory of Caesar ; those who wish to know what the liberal writers had to say about it need only to read what they said about Catiline."

Another myth which seemed to be alive to many of Machiavelli's contemporaries, along with the Church and Empire, was the sovereign city-state. Machiavelli loved his native Florence almost as much as he loved Italy, and he served the republic of Florence in diplomatic matters with incomparable zeal and integrity for about fifteen years. But he knew well enough that the free Italian city-states—here you have his own words, " where all is for the good of all "—were but a memory cherished by the heart ; he knew that their republican power had crumbled almost everywhere into the hands and estates of a few influential families who later were to become sovereigns.

There remained only the " grandi," the aristocrats. What did he think of them ? Again you have his words : " We call aristocrats all those who live idle on the rent of their enormous estates, without need of working. These people make mischief all over the republic and province ; but the most noxious are those who also have castles, and subjects to obey them ; the kingdom of Naples, the territory of Rome, Romagna, Lombardy are ridden with them ; that is the reason why there has never been either a republic or a political organization in those provinces—because this breed of men is opposed to all civilization."

Such independence of spirit, such genius for criticism, could easily have developed into a destructive force. But, although Machiavelli rejects scholasticism and its like, although he puts theology and mystical philosophy aside, he retains political science, founded on history and his own observation, a science which consists of these essential principles : it is the capacity of the human soul which makes history ; interests and passions may change in appearance, but not the law of history ; and though some nations progress and others decline, the contributions of each endure.

This is Hegelian — more than three centuries before Hegel.

A self-made man in some respects, Machiavelli was less cultured than Ariosto or many of his contemporaries, such as his aristocratic friend Guicciardini, Cardinal Bembo, Aretino, Berni, Folengo. But this lack also served to aid him in his struggle for spiritual freedom. Dante's divine dream of the *due soli*—the twin suns, Emperor and Pope, regulating the world together—did not touch Machiavelli, who believed more in the smiling scepticism of his fellow-citizen Boccaccio than in the melancholy genius of Alighieri. Machiavelli's starting-point in political ideas is an entirely negative declaration : the Middle Ages have brought anarchy ; let the state be the new emperor.

To Machiavelli's mind the state had neither a moral nor a religious task to perform ; not that he denied these elements, but he considered them social forces which should find their balance within the framework of the State. Furthermore, he considered himself a moral authority (inasmuch as he was unable to be an active political one), when he wrote : " The duty of an honest man is to teach others the good which the iniquities of the times and the inequalities of opportunity have thwarted him in doing, hoping that others capable of doing good, and with the necessary opportunity at their command will be fortunate enough to succeed."

And how does Machiavelli see the State ?

His state is the nation. " No province," he says, " can be secure and contented unless it forms part of a republic or realm." He is the first European to state the need of nations for an independent life, a bulwark against the anarchy of feudal society and—for Italy—against the covetousness of the *condottieri* and the intrigues of the popes. Up to this time no one had dared to challenge or contradict Dante, who, in his book *De Monarchia*, offered the people only one single possibility for happiness : one emperor, master of a universal monarchy, respectful to the Pope of Rome, but independent of him. The concept of independent nations had also been ruled out by the Council of Constance and, after Machiavelli, by the

Council of Trent, which adopted this contrary proposition :
" A multitude of monarchies is like a negation of God's oneness.
Because there is only one master in heaven, there ought to be
only one master on earth."

In his concern for Italy—which had been unable to unite
politically, thus following France and Spain, and all because
the Pope's political aims did not coincide with a strong Italy—
Machiavelli, three centuries before Mazzini,[1] had intuitively
conceived of national unity, stripped of the Roman heritage
which considered Italy the " *giardin dell' Impero* "—the garden
of the empire. Above all, Machiavelli wanted to rid political
life of the deadweight idea of the World Empire, and to confront his compatriots with living reality.

(It would be most unfair to reproach Machiavelli with not
having forseen that the accumulating insanities and crimes of
pseudo-nationalism would by the twentieth century unleash
two catastrophic wars on Europe, with universal repercussions.
After all, the " nationalism " of the Third Reich and the
Fascism of Italy are a downright falsification of true national
patriotism, which was formulated first by Machiavelli, then
both preached and put into reality by Mazzini and Cavour in
the nineteenth century. Furthermore, the day will come when
we who feel that we are the heirs of Machiavelli's ideas—
broadened and made more generous by Mazzini's vision—will
have to defend the wealth and fertility of national states,
encircled within the framework of a federated Europe, against
the crimes which the demagogues, thinking only of themselves
but yelling in the name of the " State," have committed under
cover of their pseudo-nationalist theories.)

We must not forget that it was because of the growth of
new nations, such as Machiavelli envisioned and Mazzini
preached, that the absolute monarchies of the past—fortresses
of privilege and licence—perished one after the other.

But it has always been the same : a principle, an idea (a
myth, if you wish), present within an historical period, renders
radical service to the progress of human liberty—to human
progress itself. But radical as the idea may be, changing concepts and even life itself, it must itself be continuously transformed in order the better to serve the concepts and new life

[1] Cf. No. 8. *The Living Thoughts of Mazzini* presented by Ignazio Silone.

provoked by it. Thus transformed, it could continue its rich life of propulsion and fruitfulness. But too often it attempts to live in its past glory ; new generations continue to reverence it until the day they discover that the idea has become mere form. In 1939, on the morning following the outbreak of the war which had been criminally foisted on the world by two dictators, Fascism—which has been responsible for an awful reversion of civilization by taking advantage of unhealthy nationalism—almost made some of the noblest spirits of Europe forget that the most clear-sighted apostles of the idea of nationalism in the nineteenth century never thought of nations as ends in themselves.

In the midst of his struggle for a united Italy, Mazzini steadily maintained that the construction of nations into complete and independent states—such as Machiavelli wished—should be but a step towards the larger union of Europe. It is not strange at all that Machiavelli did not express this idea, although undoubtedly he was aware of it. Formulated at the moment when such a large number of honest men were still dreaming of the continuation of the Roman Empire—an idea which Machiavelli considered both empty and decrepit—a wider concept of federation would have fortified the old rotten catafalque which still attracted too many Italians. Nothing on earth would have persuaded Machiavelli to look backward : the fate of Lot's wife filled him with horror.

But Machiavelli often declared in his *Discourses* that even a great united formation of states could not avoid periodic crises and internal decay—such as Spain had to endure one century after his death. Machiavelli knew that the permanent vitality of a state rests on something higher than its mere national form. Resolutely turning his eyes away from heaven, on which the Middle Ages had so long fixed its gaze, Machiavelli was none the less religious in the divine sense of the word. He was religious, even while he longed to be only rational and experimental, because he felt that by destroying this myth—in which the Italians were hopelessly enmeshed — he served the cause of right and liberty, the principles which constantly ennoble the lives of all human beings, just as religion does in its essential . elements.

(Since the rise of Fascism in their countries, certain Italian and German writers have produced books to prove that Machiavelli was above all a partisan of strong government. This has been their way of courting the gang in power, and thereby soliciting favours and jobs. There are also a few of this ilk in France, more capable, but not less despicable than their Italian and German colleagues, who at least have the poor excuse that there is no other way of feeding their families than by prostituting their pens.)

Naturally, Machiavelli is never pathetic ; neither his modesty nor his pride would allow him to be. Nor does he give himself the airs of an authority ; he expresses his deepest observations and thoughts casually (his readers need merely to understand them) and briefly. But there is one essential idea which he reiterates, and that is the necessity for freedom by which, and only by which, the life of a nation can be guaranteed. From hundreds of quotations I choose one, typical of his style, which is at once direct and indirect : " In my opinion, those who condemn the riots between noblemen and plebeians blame the very things which first produced the freedom of Rome ; they lend more importance to the noise and scoldings which emerge out of these riots than to the good effects which the tumults bring forth."

Contrary to the conclusions of the dictators' hired hacks, Machiavelli, whose only fault consisted in being too intelligent, in interpreting the soul of his time too clearly, in perceiving it with too much lucidity and recording it with too much truth, remains one of the apostles of the idea of liberty.

If the foregoing picture of Machiavelli is really the true one, why is it that such dubious posthumous fame was attached to his name for a long time—why could it give rise to the term " Machiavellism," which is synonymous with political immorality ?

The answer to this question is contained in *The Prince*, a slender volume concocted during off-hours while Machiavelli composed his life's work. However, this booklet, conceived and embellished for the purpose of pleasing a generous patron, is so full of dramatic vigour and the sharp vision which characterizes all Machiavelli's writing, that it still reads like a detective story. What wonder then that the self-styled historians of all times and countries have devoured its three-score pages,

while the same scriveners have felt rebuffed, both by the
scope and the lack of a conventional plan, by Machiavelli's
truly great work : *Discourses on the First Ten Books of Titus
Livius.*

Indeed, it was *The Prince* which made Machiavelli both
famous and infamous. And because he lived in rather dark
times, and was not given to colouring—on the contrary he was
truthful, wise and unmistakably clear, a diagnostician of modern
scope, more, the very first scholar of political science, and its
discoverer—it was not only easy but tempting for many an
adept in politics to display his none-too-clean armour with
contempt against so black a background. Actually, the real
background was the Renaissance, but who would undertake
to fight against a whole period ? It seemed less confusing and
more glorious to fight and write against one man who was
conveniently both mute and yet sufficiently alive centuries
after his death to be significant.

But why so vehement a fight ? Machiavelli, especially in
his *Prince*, promulgated the idea of political success at all costs.
Now the urge either to achieve or maintain success slumbers
in almost every man. He may believe that all means are
justifiable if only they serve this purpose. After he has read
The Prince he can no longer believe this. The soberness and
forceful logic with which Machiavelli demonstrates the necessity
for intrigue, cruelty and even murder as the means—inevitable
means—of political success, annihilates justification, reveals it
as a goal no decent man or assembly of men can consider and
still lay claim to decency. Blame oneself ? Not if one can
blame the diagnostician ! Cassandra is always murdered.

For instance, there are the Jesuits ; they inaugurated the war
against Machiavelli, burned him in effigy, forced the Pope to
put his work in the Index. But let us judge their case, if at all,
by Pascal's *Provinciales*.[1] On the Protestant side we had the case
of Frederick II of Prussia and his *Anti-Machiavel*, which is,
however, no longer a case to the unprejudiced historian.

One single quotation will be sufficient to demonstrate that
" Machiavellism " is present in highly reputed authors such as
Montesquieu : " The right of natural defence sometimes
involves the necessity to attack, if one nation notices that a

[1] Cf. No. 15. *The Living Thoughts of Pascal* presented by François Mauriac.

longer lasting peace would put another one in the position to destroy her, and if the attack is at that moment the only means to avoid that destruction." [1]

And why should we keep it a secret that Louis XIV himself slipped this piece of advice into his *Maximes pour le Dauphin* : "In every treaty, insert a clause which can easily be violated, so that the entire agreement can be broken in case the interests of the State make it expedient to do so."

" Machiavellism " in the court of Versailles ? No, merely the political law of the period, which—to judge from the Fascist government's invasion of Abyssinia in 1935 and from the action of the democratic governments in 1938 when France abandoned Czecho-Slovakia—seems to have remained unchanged even in our time. The maxims of *The Prince* echo the reality of the fifteenth century from both sides of the Alps.

In a letter written on December 10, 1513, to Francesco Vettori [2] Machiavelli described how the idea of writing *The Prince*—an idea which he characterizes as one of his " ghiribizzi " —an Italian word which might be translated as " whims "— came into his mind. Yet Machiavelli was not modest. He speaks of what he considers his real work in quite another tone.

Yes, *The Prince* is the child of Machiavelli's whim, and, though wise and brilliant, it is an off-hour product, offered on a salver. A scholar and desk-bound politician is hungry and desperately eager to re-enter the political arena : he interrupts his work on a precious opus, draws a kind of excerpt from it, a pamphlet which is to bear the title *The Prince*, and then sets out to dedicate it to one of the men in power, a prince, who— the author fervently hopes—will repay him in princely fashion with silver and situation.

Machiavelli began his great work, the *Discourses on the First Ten Books of Titus Livius*, in 1512. He finished it in 1522. *The Prince* was begun in 1513 and finished in 1516. It treats of the same theme as the *Discourses* : only *The Prince* is specific where the *Discourses* are general. If Machiavelli had not been poor and frustrated he would have written only one book on

---

[1] *De l'Esprit des Lois*, Book X, chapter II.
[2] The essential passage is reproduced on page 103.

the science of politics : the *Discourses*. The ideas contained in *The Prince* would have been incorporated into the *Discourses*. At any rate, we suggest that the student of Machiavelli regard *The Prince* simply as a part of the *Discourses*.[1]

Livy, the soil from which our tree sprang, was born in the year 59 B.C. in Padua ; he died there in A.D. 17. His fame rests upon a history of Rome, consisting of one hundred and forty-two volumes. It is a patriotic history, a glorification of the Roman mind and virtues ; throughout antiquity Titus Livius' history was valued as the authentic documentation of Augustan culture and as the apex of historical writing.

To point out to his contemporaries how far they had strayed from the glorious path of their forbears, more, " to draw mankind from the evils caused by proud indolence and lack of real historical knowledge," Machiavelli, the patriot, wrote his *Discourses* on the first ten books only of Titus Livius' one hundred and forty-two, in order " to facilitate their proper understanding." Machiavelli, the scholar and political genius, however, thereby developed the first and greatest textbook on political science.

Quite understandably, he views all greatness in history as a republican achievement—particularly a Roman republican achievement. Yet *The Prince*, as its title indicates, is monarchistic. Therefore narrowness of mind reproached Machiavelli for ambiguity : dedicate *The Prince* to Giuliano de' Medici, a pope's nephew, and the *Discourses* to the people—Machiavellism ! But scientists the world over still do the same thing every day. They develop a formula for a cure, but for some it is poison ; they draw blue prints for a new machine which may free men from labour, but only a few purses are fattened ; they submit an invention to the tycoon who financed their research, hoping in their hearts that humanity may be benefited.

The *Discourses* are not hard reading. On the contrary, while reading them one feels as if one were in the company of a hospitable, wise, benign, though unfaltering man of conviction. You do not feel that you are being instructed—only that you are being taken into his confidence.

Yet Machiavelli, the man, and everything that concerns him,

[1] In the present volume *The Prince*—minus certain repetitions—becomes a part of them. We dare to assume that Machiavelli would have approved.

becomes still clearer and more familiar when we look beyond *The Prince* and the *Discourses*. For Machiavelli not only wrote politics ; he did other things, and he also lived a life.

His public and private life was marked by an ironic pride which despised the flatteries of his age ; simplicity and naturalness of behaviour—revealed in his private letters—motivated him. His was a way of living which the *Piagnoni* (puritans) of the time of Savonarola looked upon as diseased.

He loved his comedies and verses—and he was right about his comedies : *Mandragola*, in its own way at any rate, is a masterpiece. Here you have his apology for writing it :

> Scusatelo con questo, che s'ingegna
> Con questi van pensieri
> Fare el suo tristo tempo più süave,
> Perch' altrove non have
> Dove voltare el viso ;
> Chè gli è stato interciso   .
> Monstrar con altre imprese altra virtù.

[You should excuse it—as he is trying with these frivolous thoughts to make his mournful days less bitter—he has nowhere else to turn his gaze—since it has been denied him—to show a different talent in achievements of a different sort.] " Virtù " in this sense, is not " virtue " ; the Italian word in the sixteenth century did not have the moral qualifications which we associate with it nowadays ; it meant rather the forces and qualities of a man.

The verses are bad, but they are heart-rending. Machiavelli laughed in order not to weep ; Charles VIII invaded Italy— the " grandi " did not succeed in uniting—and the Florentine secretary advised in vain, warned in vain. . . .

To really evaluate a man, one must see him in the midst of his family. In this volume you should read the letter—full of the gentlest mockery and deepest love—which his wife Marietta wrote to Machiavelli on the 24th of November 1503 : " He [our child] looks like you : skin white as snow and a head like black velvet, and hairy all over, the way you are ! Since he is so like you I suppose I must call him handsome. . . ." You should read the last letter of the *Private Letters* collection—the one in which Machiavelli's son Piero informs a relative in Pisa of his father's death : " *Lasciossi confessare le sue peccata da frate Matteo.*" [He allowed Brother Matteo to hear his confession.] The word " allowed " makes us feel that he agreed to that ceremony only out of a feeling of love for his family. His son adds : " Our father left us in direst poverty—*in somma povertà.*"

Count Sforza has had selected and arranged the
essence of Machiavelli's thought from

DISCOURSES ON THE FIRST TEN BOOKS OF
TITUS LIVIUS

THE PRINCE

PRIVATE LETTERS

THE WORKS OF

NICCOLÒ MACHIAVELLI

(1469–1527)

Discourses on the First Ten Books of Titus Livius (1512–1522)
The Prince (1513–1516)
Annals of Italy (1504)
Life of Castruccio (1520)
Art of War (1520)
History of Florence (unfinished) (1520)
Mandragola (a comedy) (printed 1524)
Clizia (a comedy)
Comedy in Prose (untitled)
Belfagor (a novel)

WHEN WE CONSIDER THE GENERAL RESPECT FOR ANTIQUITY, and how often—to say nothing of other examples— a great price is paid for some fragments of an antique statue, which we are anxious to possess to ornament our houses with, or to give to artists who strive to imitate them in their own works ; and when we see, on the other hand, the wonderful examples which the history of ancient kingdoms and republics presents to us, the prodigies of virtue and wisdom displayed by the kings, captains, citizens, and legislators who have sacrificed themselves for their country—when we see these, I say, more admired than imitated, or so much neglected that not the least trace of this ancient virtue remains, we cannot but be at the same time as much surprised as afflicted. The more so as in the differences which arise between citizens, or in the maladies to which they are subjected, we see these same people have recourse to the judgments and the remedies prescribed by the ancients. The civil laws are in fact nothing but decisions given by their jurisconsults, and which, reduced to a system, direct our modern jurists in their decisions. And what is the science of medicine but the experience of ancient physicians, which their successors have taken for their guide ? And yet to found a republic, maintain states, to govern a kingdom, organize an army, conduct a war, dispense justice, and extend empires, you will find neither prince, nor republic, nor captain, nor citizen, who has recourse to the examples of antiquity ! This neglect, I am persuaded, is due less to the weakness to which the vices of our education have reduced the world, than to the evils caused by proud indolence and to the lack of real knowledge of history, and its spirit.

Wishing, therefore, so far as in me lies, to draw mankind from this error, I have thought it proper to write upon all those matters which, after a comparison between the ancient and modern events, may seem to me necessary to facilitate their proper understanding.

I have not set off this work with pompous phrases, nor filled it with high-sounding and magnificent words, nor with any other allurements or extrinsic embellishments with which many are wont to adorn their works ; for I wished that mine should derive credit only from the truth of the matter, and that the importance of the subject should make it acceptable.

And I hope it may not be accounted presumption if a man of lowly and humble station ventures to discuss and direct the conduct of princes ; for as those who wish to delineate countries place themselves low in the plain to observe the form and character of mountains and high places, and for the purpose of studying the nature of the low country place themselves high upon an eminence, so one must be a prince to know well the character of the people, and to understand well the nature of a prince one must be of the people. In this way those who read my remarks may derive those advantages which should be the aim of all study of history ; and although the undertaking is difficult, I hope to carry it sufficiently far, so that but little may remain for others to carry it to its destined end.

OF THE BEGINNING OF CITIES IN GENERAL, AND ESPECIALLY THAT OF THE CITY OF ROME

Those who read what the beginning of Rome was, and what her lawgivers and her organization, will not be astonished that so much virtue should have maintained itself during so many centuries. To speak first of her origin, we will premise that all cities are founded either by natives of the country or by strangers. The little security which the natives found in living dispersed ; the impossibility for each to resist isolated, either because of the situation or because of their small number, the attacks of any enemy that might present himself ; the difficulty of uniting in time for defence at his approach, and the necessity of abandoning the greater number of their retreats, which quickly became a prize to the assailant—such were the motives that caused the first inhabitants of a country to build cities for the purpose of escaping these dangers. Thus, amongst many others were Athens and Venice ; the first was built under the authority of Theseus, who had gathered the dispersed inhabitants ; and the second owed its origin to the fact that several tribes had taken refuge on the little islands situated at the head of the Adriatic Sea, to escape from war, and from the Barbarians who after the fall of the Roman Empire had overrun Italy. These refugees of themselves, and without any prince to govern them, began to live under such laws as seemed to them best suited to maintain their new state. In this they succeeded, happily favoured by the long peace, for which they were indebted to their situation upon a sea without issue, where the people that ravaged Italy could not harass them, being without any ships.

The second case is when a city is built by strangers, subjects of a republic or of a prince, who, to relieve their states from an excessive population, or to defend a newly acquired territory which they wish to preserve without expense, send colonies there. The Romans founded many cities in this way within their empire. Sometimes cities are built by a prince, not for the purpose of living there, but merely as monuments to his glory; such was Alexandria, built by Alexander the Great.

The founders of cities either inhabit the cities of the country of which they take possession, as Moses did; or they build new ones, as was done by Aeneas. As men work either from necessity or from choice, and as it has been observed that virtue has more sway where labour is the result of necessity rather than of choice, it is a matter of consideration whether it might not be better to select for the establishment of a city a sterile region, where the people, compelled by necessity to be industrious, and therefore less given to idleness, would be more united, and less exposed by the poverty of the country to occasions for discord; as was the case with Ragusa, and several other cities that were built upon an ungrateful soil.

Now, as people cannot make themselves secure except by being powerful, it is necessary in the founding of a city to avoid a sterile country. As to the idleness which the fertility of a country tends to encourage, the laws should compel men to labour where the sterility of the soil does not do it.

When Alexander the Great wished to build a city, his architect, Dinocrates, pointed out to him how he could build a city on Mount Athos, which place he said, besides being very strong, could be so arranged as to give the city the appearance of the human form, which would make it a wonder worthy of the greatness of its founder. Alexander having asked him what the inhabitants were to live upon, he replied, " That I have not thought of " ; at which Alexander smiled, and, leaving Mount Athos as it was, built Alexandria, where the inhabitants would be glad to remain on account of the richness of the country and the advantages which the proximity of the Nile and the sea afforded them.

If we accept the opinion that Aeneas was the founder of Rome, then we must count that city as one of those built by strangers ; but if Romulus is taken as its founder, then must it be classed with those built by the natives of the country. Either way it will be seen that Rome was from the first free and independent ; and we shall also see (as we shall show further on) to how many privations the laws of Romulus, of Numa, and of others subjected its inhabitants ; so that neither the fertility of the soil, nor the proximity of the sea, nor their many victories, nor the greatness of the Empire, could corrupt them during several centuries, and they maintained there more virtues than have ever been seen in any other republic.

The great things which Rome achieved, and of which Titus Livius has preserved the memory, have been the work either of the government or of private individuals ; and as they relate either to the affairs of the interior or of the exterior, I shall begin to discourse of those internal operations of the government which I believe to be most noteworthy, and shall point out their results.

OF THE DIFFERENT KINDS OF REPUBLICS, AND OF WHAT KIND THE ROMAN REPUBLIC WAS

I will leave aside what might be said of cities which from their very birth have been subject to a foreign power, and will speak only of those whose origin has been independent, and which from the first governed themselves by their own laws, whether as republics or as principalities, and whose constitution and laws have differed as their origin. Some have had at the very beginning, or soon after, a legislator, who, like Lycurgus with the Lacedaemonians, gave them by a single act all the laws they needed. It is a great good fortune for a republic to have a legislator sufficiently wise to give her laws so regulated that, without the necessity of correcting them, they afford security to those who live under them. Sparta observed her laws for more than eight hundred years without altering them and without experiencing a single dangerous disturbance. Unhappy, on the contrary, is that republic which, not having at the beginning fallen into the hands of a sagacious and skilful legislator, is herself obliged to reform her laws. More unhappy still is that republic which from the first has diverged from a good constitution. And that republic is furthest from it whose vicious institutions impede her progress, and make her leave the right path that leads to a good end; for those who are in that condition can hardly ever be brought into the right road. Those republics, on the other hand, that started without having even a perfect constitution, but made a fair beginning, and are capable of improvement—such republics, I say, may perfect themselves by the aid of events. It is very true, however, that such reforms are never effected without danger, for the majority of men never willingly adopt any new law tending to change the constitution of the State unless the necessity of the change is clearly demonstrated; and as such a necessity cannot make itself felt without being accompanied with danger, the republic may easily be destroyed before having perfected its constitution.

Having proposed to myself to treat of the kind of government established at Rome, and of the events that led to its perfection, I must at the beginning observe that some of the writers on politics distinguished three kinds of government, viz. the monarchical, the aristocratic, and the democratic; and maintain that the legislators of a people must choose from these three the one that seems to them most suitable. Other authors, wiser according to the opinion of many, count six kinds of governments, three of which are very bad, and three good in themselves, but so liable to be corrupted that they become absolutely bad. The three good ones are those which we have just named; the three bad ones result from the degradation of the other three, and each of them resembles its corresponding original, so that the transition from the one to the other is very easy. Thus monarchy becomes tyranny; aristocracy degenerates into oligarchy ; and the popular government lapses readily into licentiousness. No precautions can prevent either one of the three that are reputed good, from degenerating into its opposite kind ; so great are in these the attractions and re-semblances between the good and the evil.

Chance has given birth to these different kinds of government amongst men ; for at the beginning of the world the inhabitants were few in number, and lived for a time dispersed, like beasts. As the human race increased, the necessity for uniting themselves for defence made itself felt ; the better to attain this object, they chose the strongest and most courageous from amongst themselves and placed him at their head, promising to obey him. Thence they began to know the good and the honest, and to distinguish them from the bad and vicious. They set to work to make laws, and to institute punishments for those who contravened them. Such was the origin of justice. But when they began to make sovereignty hereditary and non-elective, the children quickly degenerated from their fathers ; and, so far from trying to equal their virtues, they considered that a prince had nothing else to do than to excel all the rest in luxury, indulgence, and every other variety of pleasure. The prince consequently soon drew upon himself the general hatred. An object of hatred, he naturally felt fear ; fear in turn dictated to him precautions and wrongs, and thus tyranny quickly developed itself. Such were the beginning and causes of disorders, conspiracies, and plots against the sovereigns, set on foot, not by the feeble and timid, but by those citizens who, surpassing the others in grandeur of soul, in wealth, and in courage, could not submit to the outrages and excesses of their princes.

These, abhorring the very name of prince, constituted them-selves a new government ; and at first, bearing in mind the past tyranny, they governed in strict accordance with the laws which they had established themselves ; preferring public interests to their own, and to administer and protect with greatest care both public and private affairs. The children succeeded their fathers, and ignorant of the changes of fortune, having never experienced its reverses, soon caused the aristo-cratic government to degenerate into an oligarchic tyranny, regardless of all civil rights. They soon, however, experienced the same fate as the first tyrant; the people, disgusted with their government, placed themselves at the command of whoever was willing to attack them, and this disposition soon produced an avenger, who was sufficiently well seconded to destroy them. A popular government was therefore resolved upon, and it was so organized that the authority should not again fall into the hands of a prince or a small number of nobles. And as all governments are at first looked up to with some degree of reverence, the popular State also maintained itself for a time, though it was never of long duration, and lasted generally only about as long as the generation that had established it; for it soon ran into that kind of licence which inflicts injury upon public as well as private interests. They returned anew to the government of a prince, and from this they generally lapsed again into anarchy, step by step, in the same manner and from the same causes as we have indicated.

Such is the circle which all republics are destined to run through. Seldom, however, do they come back to the original form of government, which results from the fact that their duration is not sufficiently long to be able to undergo these repeated changes and preserve their existence. I say, then, that all kinds of government are defective; those three which we have qualified as good because they are too short-lived, and the three bad ones because of their inherent viciousness. Thus sagacious legislators, knowing the vices of each of these systems of government by themselves, have chosen one that should partake of all of them.

Amongst those justly celebrated for having established such a constitution, Lycurgus beyond doubt merits the highest praise. He organized the government of Sparta in such manner that, in giving to the king, the nobles, and the people each their portion of authority and duties, he created a government which maintained itself for over eight hundred years in the most perfect tranquillity, and reflected infinite glory upon this legislator. On the other hand, the constitution given by Solon to the Athenians, by which he established only a popular government, was of such short duration that before his death he saw the tyranny of Pisistratus arise.

But let us come to Rome. Although she had no legislator

like Lycurgus, who constituted her government, at her very origin, in a manner to secure her liberty for a length of time, yet the disunion which existed between the Senate and the people produced such extraordinary events, that chance did for her what the laws had failed to do. Thus, if Rome did not attain the first degree of happiness, she at least had the second. Her first institutions were doubtless defective, but they were not in conflict with the principles that might bring her to perfection. For Romulus and all the other kings gave her many and good laws, well suited even to a free people; but as the object of these princes was to found a monarchy, and not a republic, Rome, upon becoming free, found herself lacking all those institutions that are most essential to liberty, which her kings had not established. And although these kings lost their empire, for the reasons and in the manner which we have explained, yet those who expelled them appointed immediately two consuls in place of the king; and thus it was found that they had banished the title of king from Rome, but not the regal power. The government, composed of Consuls and a Senate, had but two of the three elements of which we have spoken, the monarchical and the aristocratic; the popular power was wanting. In the course of time, however, the insolence of the nobles, produced by the causes which we shall see further on, induced the people to rise against the others. The nobility, to save a portion of their power, were forced to yield a share of it to the people. It was then that the Tribunes of the people were created, which strengthened and confirmed the republic, being now composed of the three elements of which we have spoken above. Fortune favoured her, so that, although the authority passed successively from the kings and nobles to the people, by the same degrees and for the same reasons that we have spoken of, yet the royal authority was never entirely abolished to bestow it upon the nobles; and these were never entirely deprived of their authority to give it to the people; but a combination was formed of the three powers, which rendered the constitution perfect.

OF THE EVENTS THAT MADE THE REPUBLIC
MORE PERFECT

All those who have written upon civil institutions demonstrate (and history is full of examples to support them) that whoever desires to found a State and give it laws must start with assuming that all men are bad and ever ready to display their vicious nature, whenever they may find occasion for it. If their evil disposition remains concealed for a time, it must be attributed to some unknown reason; and we must assume that it lacked occasion to show itself; but time, which has been said to be the father of all truth, does not fail to bring it to light. After the expulsion of the Tarquins the greatest harmony seemed to prevail between the Senate and the people. The nobles seemed to have laid aside all their haughtiness and assumed popular manners, which made them supportable even to the lowest of the citizens. After the death of the Tarquins, being no longer under the influence that had restrained them, the nobles determined to establish a new order of things, which had the same effect as the misrule of the Tarquins during their existence; and therefore, after many troubles, tumults, and dangers occasioned by the excesses which both the nobles and the people committed, they came, for the security of the people, to the creation of the Tribunes, who were endowed with so many prerogatives, and surrounded with so much respect, that they formed a powerful barrier between the Senate and the people, which curbed the insolence of the former.

THE DISUNION OF THE SENATE AND THE PEOPLE RENDERS
THE REPUBLIC OF ROME POWERFUL AND FREE

I shall not pass over in silence the disturbances that occurred in Rome from the time of the death of the Tarquins to that or the creation of the Tribunes; and shall afterwards refute the opinion of those who claim that the Roman republic has always been a theatre of turbulence and disorder, and that if its extreme good fortune and the military discipline had not supplied the defects of her constitution, she would have deserved the lowest rank amongst the republics.

I maintain that those who blame the quarrels of the Senate and the people of Rome condemn that which was the very origin of liberty, and that they were probably more impressed by the cries and noise which these disturbances occasioned in the public places than by the good effect which they produced; and that they do not consider that in every republic there are two parties, that of the nobles and that of the people; and all the laws that are favourable to liberty result from the opposition of these parties to each other. Nor can we regard a republic as disorderly where so many virtues were seen to shine. For good examples are the result of good education, and good education is due to good laws; and good laws in their turn spring from those very agitations which have been so inconsiderately condemned by many. For whoever will carefully examine the result of these agitations will find that they have neither caused exiles nor any violence prejudicial to the general good, and will be convinced even that they have given rise to laws that were to the advantage of public liberty. And if it be said that these are strange means—to hear constantly the cries of the people furious against the Senate, and of a Senate declaiming against the people, to see the populace rush tumultuously through the streets, close their houses, and even leave the city of Rome—I reply, that all these things can alarm only those who read of them, and that every free State ought to afford the people the opportunity of giving vent, so to say, to their ambition; and above all those republics which on important occasions have to avail themselves of this very people. "The people," says Cicero, "although ignorant, yet are capable of appreciating the truth, and yield to it readily when it is presented to them by a man whom they esteem worthy of their confidence."

If the troubles of Rome occasioned the creation of Tribunes, then they cannot be praised too highly; for besides giving to the people a share in the public administration, these Tribunes were established as the most assured guardians of Roman liberty.

TO WHOM CAN THE GUARDIANSHIP OF LIBERTY MORE SAFELY BE CONFIDED, TO THE NOBLES OR TO THE PEOPLE ? AND WHICH OF THE TWO HAVE MOST CAUSE FOR CREATING DISTURBANCES, THOSE WHO WISH TO ACQUIRE, OR THOSE WHO DESIRE TO CONSERVE ?

All the legislators that have given wise constitutions to republics have deemed it an essential precaution to establish a guard and protection to liberty ; and according as this was more or less wisely placed, liberty endured a greater or less length of time. As every republic was composed of nobles and people, the question arose into whose hands it was best to confide the protection of liberty. The Lacedaemonians, and in our day the Venetians, gave it into the hands of the nobility ; but the Romans entrusted it to the people. We must examine, therefore, which of these republics made the best choice. I will say that one should always confide any deposit to those who have least desire of violating it ; and doubtless, if we consider the objects of the nobles and of the people, we must see that the first have a great desire to dominate, whilst the latter have only the wish not to be dominated, and consequently a greater desire to live in the enjoyment of liberty ; so that when the people are entrusted with the care of any privilege or liberty, being less disposed to encroach upon it, they will of necessity take better care of it ; and being unable to take it away themselves, will prevent others from doing so.

On the contrary, it is said, in favour of the course adopted by Sparta and Venice, that the preference given to the nobility, as guardians of public liberty, has two advantages : the first, to yield something to the ambition of those who, being more engaged in the management of public affairs, find, so to say, in the weapon which the office places in their hands, a means of power that satisfies them ; the other, to deprive the restless spirit of the masses of an authority calculated from its very nature to produce trouble and dissensions, and apt to drive the nobles to some act of desperation, which in time may cause the greatest misfortunes.

And truly, whoever weighs all these reasons accurately may well remain in doubt which of the two classes he would choose as the guardians of liberty, not knowing which would be least dangerous—those who seek to acquire an authority which they have not, or those who desire to preserve that which they already possess. It seems, however, that great troubles are most frequently occasioned by those who possess ; for the fear to lose stirs the same passions in men as the desire to gain, as men do not believe themselves sure of what they already possess except by acquiring still more ; and, moreover, these new acquisitions are so many means of strength and power for abuses ; and what is still worse is that the haughty manners and insolence of the nobles and the rich excite in the breasts of those who have neither birth nor wealth, not only the desire to possess them, but also the wish to revenge themselves by depriving the former of those riches and honours which they see them employ so badly.

SHOWING HOW NECESSARY THE FACULTY OF ACCUSATION IS IN A REPUBLIC FOR THE MAINTENANCE OF LIBERTY

No more useful and necessary authority can be given to those who are appointed as guardians of liberty than the faculty of accusing the citizens to the people, or to any magistrate or council, for any attempt against public liberty. Such a system has two very marked advantages for a republic. The first is, that the apprehension of being accused prevents the citizens from attempting anything against the State, and should they nevertheless attempt it, they are immediately punished, without regard to persons. The other is, that it affords a way for those evil dispositions that arise in one way or another against some one citizen to vent themselves ; and when these ferments cannot in some way exhaust themselves, their promoters are apt to resort to some extraordinary means, that may lead to the ruin of the republic. Nothing, on the other hand, renders a republic more firm and stable, than to organize it in such a way that the excitement of the ill-humours that agitate a State may have a way prescribed by law for venting itself.

This can be demonstrated by many examples, and particularly by that of Coriolanus, which Titus Livius mentions, where he says that the Roman nobility was much irritated against the people, because they believed that the people had obtained too much authority by the creation of the Tribunes who defended them ; and as Rome at the time was suffering greatly from want of provisions, and the Senate had sent to Sicily for supplies of grain, Coriolanus, who was a declared enemy of the popular faction, suggested to the Senate that it afforded a favourable opportunity for them to chastise the people, and to deprive them of the authority they had acquired and assumed to the prejudice of the nobility, by not distributing the grain, and thus keeping the people in a famished condition. When this proposition came to the ears of the people, it excited so great an indignation against Coriolanus, that, on coming out of the Senate, he would have been killed in a tumultuary manner if the Tribunes had not summoned him to appear before them and defend his cause. This occurrence shows, as we have said above, how useful and necessary it is for a republic to have laws that afford to the masses the opportunity of giving vent to the hatred they may have conceived against any citizen ; for if there exist no legal means for this, they will resort to illegal ones, which beyond doubt produce much worse effects. For ordinarily when a citizen is oppressed, and even if an injustice is committed against him, it rarely causes any disturbance in the republic ; for this oppression has been effected by neither private nor foreign forces, which are most destructive to public liberty, but is effected solely by the public force of the State in accordance with the established laws, which have their prescribed limits that cannot be transcended to the injury of the republic.

IN PROPORTION AS ACCUSATIONS ARE USEFUL IN A REPUBLIC, SO ARE CALUMNIES PERNICIOUS

Despite the courage displayed by Furius Camillus in liberating Rome from the yoke of the Gauls, which caused all the citizens of Rome to yield him the first place without deeming themselves degraded thereby, Manlius Capitolinus could not brook that so much honour and glory should be bestowed upon him ; for, having himself saved the Capitol, he considered that he had contributed as much to the salvation of Rome as Furius Camillus, and that he was in no way inferior to him in military talents. And, finding that he could not sow discord amongst the Senators, he turned to the people and spread various sinister reports amongst them. Amongst other things, he circulated a statement that the amount of money which had been collected for payment to the Gauls had never been paid over to them, but had been appropriated by some private citizens. These statements produced a great impression among the people. This greatly displeased the Senate, who, deeming the occasion momentous and perilous, created a Dictator, who should take cognizance of the facts and repress the audacity of Manlius ; whereupon the Dictator had him promptly summoned. Manlius was called upon to specify the persons who had appropriated the money in question. To this he made no particular reply, but in an evasive manner said that it was unnecessary to mention the names, as they knew them very well already ; whereupon the Dictator had him incarcerated.

This shows how much detested calumnies are in republics, as well as under any other government, and that no means should be left unemployed to repress them in time. Now, there is no more effectual way for putting an end to calumnies than to introduce the system of legal accusations, which will be as beneficial to republics as calumnies are injurious. On the other hand, there is this difference, namely, that calumnies require neither witnesses, nor confrontings, nor any particulars to prove them, so that every citizen may be calumniated by another, whilst accusations cannot be lodged against anyone without being accompanied by positive proofs and circumstances that demonstrate the truth of the accusation. Accusations must be brought before the magistrates, or the people, or the councils, whilst calumnies are spread in public places as well as in private dwellings ; and calumnies are more practised where the system of accusations does not exist, and in cities the constitution of which does not admit of them. The lawgiver of a republic, therefore, should give every citizen the right to accuse another citizen without fear or suspicion ; and this being done, and properly carried out, he should severely punish calumniators, who would have no right to complain of such punishment, it being open to them to bring charges against those whom they had in private calumniated. And where this system is not well established there will always be great disorders, for calumnies irritate, but do not chastise men ; and those who have been thus irritated will think of strengthening themselves, hating more than fearing the slanders spread against them.

TO FOUND A NEW REPUBLIC, OR TO REFORM ENTIRELY THE OLD INSTITUTIONS OF AN EXISTING ONE, MUST BE THE WORK OF ONE MAN ONLY

Many will perhaps consider it an evil example that the founder of a civil society, as Romulus was, should first have killed his brother, and then have consented to the death of Titus Tatius, who had been elected to share the royal authority with him ; from which it might be concluded that the citizens, according to the example of their prince, might, from ambition and the desire to rule, destroy those who attempt to oppose their authority. This opinion would be correct, if we do not take into consideration the object which Romulus had in view in committing that homicide. But we must assume, as a general rule, that it never or rarely happens that a republic or monarchy is well constituted, or its old institutions entirely reformed, unless it is done by only one individual ; it is even necessary that he whose mind has conceived such a constitution should be alone in carrying it into effect. A sagacious legislator of a republic, therefore, whose object is to promote the public good, and not his private interests, and who prefers his country to his own successors, should concentrate all authority in himself ; and a wise mind will never censure anyone for having employed any extraordinary means for the purpose of establishing a kingdom or constituting a republic. It is well that, when the act accuses him, the result should excuse him ; and when the result is good, as in the case of Romulus, it will always absolve him from blame. For he is to be reprehended who commits violence for the purpose of destroying, and not he who employs it for beneficent purposes.

The lawgiver should, however, be sufficiently wise and virtuous not to leave this authority which he has assumed either to his heirs or to anyone else ; for, mankind being more prone to evil than to good, his successor might employ for evil purposes the power which he had used only for good ends. Besides, although one man alone should organize a government, yet it will not endure long if the administration of it remains on the shoulders of a single individual ; it is well, then, to confide this to the charge of many, for thus it will be sustained by the many. Therefore, as the organization of anything cannot be made by many, because the divergence of their opinions hinders them from agreeing as to what is best, yet, when once they do understand it, they will not readily agree to abandon it.

The above views might be corroborated by any number of examples, such as those of Moses, Lycurgus, Solon, and other founders of monarchies and republics, who were enabled to establish laws suitable for the general good only by keeping for themselves an exclusive authority.

IN PROPORTION AS THE FOUNDERS OF A REPUBLIC OR MONARCHY ARE ENTITLED TO PRAISE SO DO THE FOUNDERS OF A TYRANNY DESERVE EXECRATION

Of all men who have been eulogized, those deserve it most who have been the authors and founders of religions ; next come such as have established republics or kingdoms. After these the most celebrated are those who have commanded armies, and have extended the possessions of their kingdom or country. To these may be added literary men, but, as these are of different kinds, they are celebrated according to their respective degrees of excellence. All others—and their number is infinite—receive such share of praise as pertains to the exercise of their arts and professions. On the contrary, those are doomed to infamy and universal execration who have destroyed religions, who have overturned republics and kingdoms, who are enemies of virtue, of letters, and of every art that is useful and honourable to mankind. Such are the impious and violent, the ignorant, the idle, the vile and degraded. And there are none so foolish or so wise, so wicked or so good, that, in choosing between these two qualities, they do not praise what is praiseworthy and blame that which deserves blame. And yet nearly all men, deceived by a false good and a false glory, allow themselves voluntarily or ignorantly to be drawn towards those who deserve more blame than praise.

Nor let anyone be deceived by the glory of that Caesar who has been so much celebrated by writers ; for those who praised him were corrupted by his fortune, and frightened by the long duration of the empire that was maintained under his name, and which did not permit writers to speak of him with freedom. And if anyone wishes to know what would have been said of him if writers had been free to speak their minds, let him read what Catiline said of him. Caesar is as much more to be condemned, as he who commits an evil deed is more guilty than he who merely has the evil intention. He will also see how highly Brutus was eulogized ; for, not being allowed to blame Caesar on account of his power, they extolled his enemy.

The history of Emperors carefully studied would prove an ample guide to any prince, and serve to show him the way to glory or to infamy, to security or to perpetual apprehension. He will furthermore learn from the lessons of that history how an empire should be organized properly ; for all the Emperors that succeeded to the throne by inheritance, except Titus, were bad, and those who became Emperors by adoption were all good, such as the five from Nero to Marcus Aurelius ; and when the Empire became hereditary, it came to ruin. Let any prince now place himself in the times from Nerva to Marcus Aurelius, and let him compare them with those that preceded and followed that period, and let him choose in which of the two he would like to have been born, and in which he would like to have reigned. In the period under the good Emperors he will see the prince secure amidst his people, who are also living in security ; he will see peace and justice prevail in the world, the authority of the Senate respected, the magistrates honoured, the wealthy citizens enjoying their riches, nobility and virtue exalted, and everywhere will he see tranquillity and well-being. And on the other hand he will behold all animosity, licence, corruption, and all noble ambitions extinct. During the period of the good Emperors he will see that golden age when everyone could hold and defend whatever opinion he pleased ; in fine, he will see the triumph of the world, the prince surrounded with reverence and glory, and beloved by his people, who are happy in their security. And truly, if a prince be anxious for glory and the good opinion of the world, he should rather wish to possess a corrupt city, not to ruin it wholly like Caesar, but to reorganize it like Romulus. For certainly the heavens cannot afford a man a greater opportunity of glory, nor could men desire a better one.

OF THE RELIGION OF THE ROMANS

Whoever reads Roman history attentively will see in how great a degree religion served in the command of the armies, in uniting the people and keeping them well conducted, and in covering the wicked with shame. So that if the question were discussed whether Rome was more indebted to Romulus or to Numa, I believe that the highest merit would be conceded to Numa ; for where religion exists it is easy to introduce armies and discipline, but where there are armies and no religion it is difficult to introduce the latter. Romulus could organize the Senate and establish other civil and military institutions without the aid of divine authority, yet it was very necessary for Numa, who feigned that he held converse with a nymph, who dictated to him all that he wished to persuade the people to. In truth, there never was any remarkable lawgiver amongst the people who did not resort to divine authority, as otherwise his laws would not have been accepted by the people ; for there are many good laws, the importance of which is known to the sagacious lawgiver, but the reasons for which are not sufficiently evident to enable him to persuade others to submit to them ; and therefore do wise men, for the purpose of removing this difficulty, resort to divine authority. Thus did Lycurgus and Solon, and many others who aimed at the same thing.

The Roman people, then, admiring the wisdom and goodness of Numa, yielded in all things to his advice. It is true that those were very religious times, and the people with whom Numa had to deal were very untutored and superstitious, which made it easy for him to carry out his designs, being able to impress upon them any new form. And doubtless, if anyone wanted to establish a republic at the present time, he would find it much easier with the simple mountaineers, than with such as are accustomed to live in cities. Yet that does not make it impossible to persuade civilized men who claim to be enlightened. The people of Florence are far from considering themselves ignorant and benighted, and yet Brother Girolamo Savonarola succeeded in persuading them that he held converse with God. I will not pretend to judge whether it was true or not, for we must speak with all respect of so great a man ; but I may well say that an immense number believed it, without having seen any extraordinary manifestations that should have made them believe it ; but it was the purity of his life, the doctrines he preached, and the subjects he selected for his discourses that sufficed to make the people have faith in him. Let no one, then, fear not to be able to accomplish what others have done, for all men are born and live and die in the same way, and therefore resemble each other.

A PEOPLE THAT HAS BEEN ACCUSTOMED TO LIVE UNDER A PRINCE PRESERVES ITS LIBERTIES WITH DIFFICULTY IF BY ACCIDENT IT HAS BECOME FREE

Many examples in ancient history prove how difficult it is for a people that has been accustomed to live under the government of a prince to preserve its liberty if by some accident it has recovered it. And this difficulty is a reasonable one ; for such a people may well be compared to some wild animal which (although by nature ferocious and savage) has been as it were subdued by having been always kept imprisoned and in servitude, and being let out into the open fields, not knowing how to provide food and shelter for itself, becomes an easy prey to the first one who attempts to chain it up again. The same thing happens to a people that has not been accustomed to self-government ; for, ignorant of all public affairs, of all means of defence or offence, neither knowing the princes nor being known by them, it soon relapses under a yoke, oftentimes much heavier than the one which it had but just shaken off.

To the above comes another difficulty, which is, that the state that becomes free makes enemies for itself and not friends. All those become its enemies who were benefited by the tyrannical abuses and fattened upon the treasures of the prince, and who, being now deprived of these advantages, cannot remain content, and are therefore driven to attempt to re-establish the tyranny, so as to recover their former authority and advantages. A state then, as I have said, that becomes free makes no friends ; for free governments bestow honours and rewards only according to certain honest and fixed rules, outside of which there are neither the one nor the other. And such as obtain these honours and rewards do not consider themselves under obligations to anyone, because they believe that they were entitled to them by their merits. Besides the advantages that result to the mass of the people from a free government, such as to be able freely to enjoy one's own without apprehension, to have nothing to fear for the honour of his wife and daughters, or for himself— all these, I say, are not appreciated by anyone whilst he is in the enjoyment of them ; for no one will confess himself under obligation to anyone merely because he has not been injured by him.

Thus it is that a state that has freshly achieved liberty makes enemies and no friends. And to prevent this inconvenience, and the disorders which are apt to come with it, there is no remedy more powerful, valid, healthful, and necessary than the killing of the sons of Brutus, who, as history shows, had conspired with other Roman youths for no other reason than because under the Consuls they could not have the same extraordinary advantages they had enjoyed under the kings ; so that the liberty of the people seemed to have become their bondage. Whoever undertakes to govern a people under the form of either republic or monarchy, without making sure of those who are opposed to this new order of things, establishes a government of very brief duration.

WHOEVER WISHES TO REFORM AN EXISTING GOVERNMENT IN A FREE STATE SHOULD AT LEAST PRESERVE THE SEMBLANCE OF THE OLD FORMS

He who desires or attempts to reform the government of a state, and wishes to have it accepted and capable of maintaining itself to the satisfaction of everybody, must at least retain the semblance of the old forms ; so that it may seem to the people that there has been no change in the institutions, even though in fact they are entirely different from the old ones. For the great majority of mankind are satisfied with appearances, as though they were realities, and are often even more influenced by the things that seem than by those that are. The Romans understood this well, and for that reason, when they first recovered their liberty, and had created two Consuls in place of a king, they would not allow these more than twelve lictors, so as not to exceed the number that had served the king. Besides this, the Romans were accustomed to an annual sacrifice that could only be performed by the king in person ; and as they did not wish that the people, in consequence of the absence of the king, should have occasion to regret the loss of any of their old customs, they created a special chief for that ceremony, whom they called the king of the sacrifice, and placed him under their high priest ; so that the people enjoyed these annual sacrificial ceremonies, and had no pretext, from the want of them, for desiring the restoration of the kings. And this rule should be observed by all who wish to abolish an existing system of government in any state and introduce a new and more liberal one. For as all novelties excite the minds of men, it is important to retain in such innovations as much as possible the previously existing forms. And if the number, authority, and duration of the term of service of the magistrates be changed, the titles at least ought to be preserved. This, as I have said, should be observed by whoever desires to convert an absolute government either into a republic or a monarchy ; but, on the contrary, he who wishes to establish at absolute power, such as ancient writers called a tyranny, must change everything.

OF NEW PRINCIPALITIES THAT HAVE BEEN ACQUIRED BY THE VALOUR OF THE PRINCE AND BY HIS OWN TROOPS [1]

Let no one wonder if, in what I am about to say of entirely new principalities and of the prince and his government, I cite the very highest examples. For as men almost always follow the beaten track of others, and proceed in their actions by imitation, and yet cannot altogether follow the ways of

[1] *The Prince.*

others, nor attain the high qualities of those whom they imitate, so a wise man should ever follow the ways of great men and endeavour to imitate only such as have been most eminent ; so that even if his merits do not quite equal theirs, yet that they may in some measure reflect their greatness. He should do as the skilful archer, who, seeing that the object he desires to hit is too distant, and knowing the extent to which his bow will carry, aims higher than the destined mark, not for the purpose, of sending his arrow to that height, but so that by this elevation it may reach the desired aim.

I say then that a new prince in an entirely new principality will experience more or less difficulty in maintaining himself, according as he has more or less courage and ability. And as such an event as to become a prince from a mere private individual presupposes either great courage or rare good fortune, it would seem that one or the other of these two causes ought in a measure to mitigate many of these difficulties. But he who depends least upon fortune will maintain himself best.

To come now to those who by their courage and ability, and not by fortune, have risen to the rank of rulers, I will say that the most eminent of such were Moses, Cyrus, Romulus, Theseus, and the like. And although we may not discuss Moses, who was a mere executor of the things ordained by God, yet he merits our admiration, if only for that grace which made him worthy to hold direct communion with the Almighty. But if we consider Cyrus and others who have conquered or founded empires, we shall find them all worthy of admiration ; for if we study their acts and particular ordinances, they do not seem very different from those of Moses, although he had so great a teacher. We shall also find in examining their acts and lives, that they had no other favour from fortune but opportunity, which gave them the material which they could mould into whatever form seemed to them best ; and without such opportunity the great qualities of their souls would have been wasted, whilst without those great qualities the opportunities would have been in vain.

It was necessary then for Moses to find the people of Israel slaves in Egypt, and oppressed by the Egyptians, so that to escape from that bondage they resolved to follow him. It was necessary that Romulus should not have been kept in

Alba, and that he should have been exposed at his birth, for him to have become the founder and king of Rome. And so it was necessary for Cyrus to find the Persians dissatisfied with the rule of the Medes, and the Medes effeminate and enfeebled by long peace. And finally, Theseus could not have manifested his courage had he not found the Athenians dispersed. These opportunities therefore made these men fortunate, and it was their lofty virtue that enabled them to recognize the opportunities by which their countries were made illustrious and most happy. Those who by similar noble conduct become princes acquire their principalities with difficulty, but maintain them with ease ; and the difficulties which they experience in acquiring their principalities arise in part from the new ordinances and customs which they are obliged to introduce for the purpose of founding their state and their own security. We must bear in mind, then, that there is nothing more difficult and dangerous, or more doubtful of success, than an attempt to introduce a new order of things in any state. For the innovator has for enemies all those who derived advantages from the old order of things, whilst those who expect to be benefited by the new institutions will be but lukewarm defenders. This indifference arises in part from the fear of their adversaries who were favoured by the existing laws, and partly from the incredulity of men who have no faith in anything new that is not the result of well-established experience. Hence it is that, whenever the opponents of the new order of things have the opportunity to attack it, they will do it with the zeal of partisans, whilst the others defend it but feebly, so that it is dangerous to rely upon the latter.

If we desire to discuss this subject thoroughly, it will be necessary to examine whether such innovators depend upon themselves, or whether they rely upon others ; that is to say, whether for the purpose of carrying out their plans they have to resort to entreaties, or whether they can accomplish it by force. In the first case they always succeed badly, and fail to conclude anything ; but when they depend upon their own strength to carry their innovations through, then they rarely incur any danger. Thence it was that all prophets who came with arms in hand were successful, whilst those who were not armed were ruined. For besides the reasons given above, the dispositions of peoples are variable ; it is easy to persuade them to anything, but difficult to confirm them in that belief. And therefore a prophet should be prepared, in case the people will not believe any more, to be able by force to compel them to that belief.

Moses, Cyrus, Theseus, and Romulus would not have been able to make their laws and institutions observed for any length of time if they had not been prepared to enforce them with arms. This was the experience of Brother Girolamo Savonarola, who failed in his attempt to establish a new order of things so soon as the multitude ceased to believe in him ; for he had not the means to keep his believers firm in their faith, nor to make the unbelievers believe. And yet these great men experienced great difficulties in their course, and met danger at every step, which could only be overcome by their courage and ability. But once having surmounted them, then they began to be held in veneration ; and having crushed those who were jealous of their great qualities, they remained powerful, secure, honoured, and happy.

A NEW PRINCE IN A CITY OR PROVINCE CONQUERED BY HIM SHOULD ORGANIZE EVERYTHING ANEW

Whoever becomes prince of a city or state, especially if the foundation of his power is feeble, and does not wish to establish there either a monarchy or a republic, will find the best means for holding that principality to organize the government entirely anew (he being himself a new prince there) ; that is, he should appoint new governors with new titles, new powers, and new men, and he should make the poor rich, as David did when he became king, " who heaped riches upon the needy, and dismissed the wealthy empty-handed." Besides this, he should destroy the old cities and build new ones, and transfer the inhabitants from one place to another ; in short, he should leave nothing unchanged in that province, so that there should be neither rank, nor grade, nor honour, nor wealth, that should not be recognized as coming from him. He should take Philip of Macedon, father of Alexander, for his model, who by proceeding in that manner became, from a petty king, master of all Greece. And his historian tells us that he transferred the inhabitants from one province to another, as shepherds move their flocks from place to place. Doubtless these means are cruel and destructive of all civilized life, and neither Christian nor even human, and should be avoided by everyone. In fact, the life of a private citizen would be preferable to that of a king at the expense of the ruin of so many human beings. Nevertheless, whoever is unwilling to adopt the first and humane course must, if he wishes to maintain his power, follow the latter evil course. But men generally decide upon a middle course, which is most hazardous; for they know neither how to be entirely good nor entirely bad.

WHICH OF THE TWO IS MOST UNGRATEFUL, A PEOPLE OR A PRINCE

It seems to me proper to examine whether the people or a prince is more liable to the charge of ingratitude; and by way of illustrating this question the better, I set out by saying that the vice of ingratitude springs either from avarice or fear. For when a people or a prince has sent a general on some important expedition where by his success he acquires great glory, the prince or people is in turn bound to reward him. But if instead of such reward they dishonour and wrong him, influenced thereto by avarice, then they are guilty of an inexcusable wrong, which will involve them in eternal infamy. And yet there are many princes who commit this wrong, for which fact Tacitus assigns the reason in the following sentence: " Men are more ready to repay an injury than a benefit, because gratitude is a burden and revenge a pleasure." We read of many instances of this kind; for the general who by his valour has conquered a state for his master, and won great glory for himself by his victory over the enemy, and has loaded his soldiers with rich booty, acquires necessarily with his own soldiers, as well as with those of the enemy and with the subjects of the prince, so high a reputation, that his very victory may become distasteful, and a cause for apprehension to his prince. The means that suggest themselves to him are either to have the general killed, or to deprive him of that reputation which he has acquired with the prince's army and the people, by using every means to prove that the general's victory was not due to his skill and courage, but to chance and the cowardice of the enemy, or to the sagacity of the other captains who were with him in that action.

Fear and suspicion are so natural to princes that they cannot defend themselves against them. If, then, a prince cannot prevent himself from committing such wrongs, it is surely no wonder, nor matter worthy of more consideration, if a people acts in a similar manner.

In concluding, I say that, as the vice of ingratitude is usually the consequence of either avarice or fear, it will be seen that peoples never fall into this error from avarice, and that fear also makes them less liable to it than princes, inasmuch as they have less reason for fear.

A REPUBLIC OR A PRINCE SHOULD NOT DEFER SECURING THE GOODWILL OF THE PEOPLE UNTIL THEY ARE THEMSELVES IN DIFFICULTIES

Although the Romans happily always treated the people with liberality, yet when danger came upon them, and Porsenna attacked Rome for the purpose of restoring the Tarquins, the Senate was doubtful whether the people might not rather accept the restoration of the kings than undergo a war ; and to assure themselves of the people, they relieved them of the impost on salt and of all other taxes, saying that the poor did enough for the public benefit in rearing their children ; and although in consequence of this liberality the people submitted to the hardships and privations of siege, famine, and war, yet let no one, trusting to this example, defer securing the goodwill of the people until the moment of danger ; for they will never succeed in it as the Romans did. For the masses will think that they do not owe the benefits you have bestowed upon them to you, but to your adversaries ; and fearing that, when the danger is past, you will again take from them what under the pressure of danger you conceded to them, they will feel under no obligations to you. The reason why this proceeding turned out well for the Romans was that the government was still new and not yet firmly established, and the people had seen that other laws had been enacted for their benefit, such, for instance, as that of the appeal to the people ; and thus they were easily persuaded that the relief from taxation which had been granted to them was not caused so much by the approach of the enemy as by the disposition of the Senate to favour them.

And as it is rare that similar circumstances concur, so it is equally rare that similar remedies avail. Therefore republics as well as princes should think in advance what adversities may befall them, and of whom they may have need in time of trouble, and then they should comport themselves towards those in the manner they might deem necessary in case danger should come upon them. And whoever acts differently, whether prince or republic, and more especially a prince, and supposes from the above-related fact that it is time enough by benefits to secure the good will of the people when danger has come upon him, deceives himself greatly ; for not only will he fail to obtain the good will of the people, but he will accelerate his own destruction.

WHEN AN EVIL HAS SPRUNG UP WITHIN A STATE, OR COME UPON IT FROM WITHOUT, IT IS SAFER TO TEMPORIZE WITH IT RATHER THAN TO ATTACK IT VIOLENTLY

When any evil arises within a republic, or threatens it from without, that is to say, from an intrinsic or extrinsic cause, and has become so great as to fill everyone with apprehension, the more certain remedy by far is to temporize with it, rather than to attempt to extirpate it ; for almost invariably he who attempts to crush it will rather increase its force, and will accelerate the harm apprehended from it. And such evils arise more frequently in a republic from intrinsic than extrinsic causes, as it often occurs that a citizen is allowed to acquire more authority than is proper ; or that changes are permitted in a law which is the very nerve and life of liberty ; and then they let this evil go so far that it becomes more hazardous to correct it than to allow it to run on. And it is the more difficult to recognize these evils at their origin, as it seems natural to men always to favour the beginning of things ; and these favours are more readily

4

accorded to such acts as seem to have some merit in them, and are done by young men. For if in a republic a noble youth is seen to rise, who is possessed of some extraordinary merits, the eyes of all citizens quickly turn to him, and all hasten to show him honour, regardless of consequences ; so that, if he is in any way ambitious, the gifts of nature and the favour of his fellow-citizens will soon raise him to such a height that, when the citizens become sensible of the error they have committed, they have no longer the requisite means for checking him, and their efforts to employ such as they have will only accelerate his advance to power.

Many instances of this might be cited, but I will confine myself to one which occurred in our own city of Florence. Cosimo de' Medici, to whom the house of Medici owes the beginning of its greatness, obtained such reputation and authority through his own sagacity and the ignorance of his fellow-citizens, that he became a cause of apprehension to the government, and the other citizens judged it hazardous to offend him, but more dangerous still to allow him to go on. At that time there lived in Florence Niccolò Uzzano, reputed a man of consummate ability in matters of state, who, having committed the first error of not foreseeing the danger that might result from the great influence of Cosimo, would never permit the Florentines, so long as he lived, to commit the second error of trying to destroy Cosimo, judging that any such attempt would lead to the ruin of the state, as in fact proved to be the case after his death. For the citizens, regardless of the counsels of Uzzano, combined against Cosimo and drove him from Florence. The consequence was that the partisans of Cosimo, to resent this insult, shortly afterwards recalled him and made him prince of the republic, which position he never would have attained but for the previous hostility manifested towards him. The same thing happened in Rome with regard to Caesar, who by his courage and merits first won the favour of Pompey and of other prominent citizens, but which favour was shortly after converted into fear ; to which Cicero testifies, saying " that Pompey had begun too late to fear Caesar." This fear caused them to think of measures of safety, which however only accelerated the ruin of the republic.

I say, then, that inasmuch as it is difficult to know these

evils at their first origin, owing to an illusion which all new things are apt to produce, the wiser course is to temporize with such evils when they are recognized, instead of violently attacking them ; for by temporizing with them they will either die out of themselves, or at least their worst results will be long deferred. And princes or magistrates who wish to destroy such evils must watch all points, and must be careful in attacking them not to increase instead of diminishing them, for they must not believe that a fire can be extinguished by blowing upon it. They should carefully examine the extent and force of the evil, and if they think themselves sufficiently strong to combat it, they should attack it regardless of consequences ; otherwise they should let it be, and in no wise attempt it.

THE AUTHORITY OF THE DICTATORSHIP HAS ALWAYS PROVED BENEFICIAL TO ROME, AND NEVER INJURIOUS ; IT IS THE AUTHORITY WHICH MEN USURP, AND NOT THAT WHICH IS GIVEN THEM BY THE FREE SUFFRAGES OF THEIR FELLOW-CITIZENS, THAT IS DANGEROUS TO CIVIL LIBERTY

Some writers have blamed those Romans who first introduced the practice of creating Dictators, as being calculated in time to lead to despotism in Rome ; alleging that the first tyrant of that city governed her under the title of Dictator, and saying that, if it had not been for this office, Caesar never could under any other public title have imposed his despotism upon the Romans. Evidently the subject could not have been thoroughly considered by those who advance this opinion, so generally adopted without good reasons ; for it was neither the name nor the rank of the Dictator that subjected Rome to servitude, but it was the authority which citizens usurped to perpetuate themselves in the government. And if the title of Dictator had not existed in Rome, some other would have been taken ; for power can easily take a name, but a name cannot give power. And it is seen that the dictatorship, whenever created according to public law and not usurped by individual authority, always proved beneficial to Rome ; it is the magistracies and powers that are created by illegitimate means which harm a republic, and not those that are appointed in the regular way, as was the case in Rome, where in the long course of time no Dictator ever failed to prove beneficial to the republic.

The reason of this is perfectly evident : first, before a citizen can be in a position to usurp extraordinary powers, many things must concur, which in a republic as yet uncorrupted never can happen ; for he must be exceedingly rich, and must have many adherents and partisans, which cannot be where the laws are observed ; and even if he had them, he would never be supported by the free suffrages of the people, for such men are generally looked upon as dangerous. Besides this, Dictators were appointed only for a limited term, and not in perpetuity, and their power to act was confined to the particular occasion for which they were created. This power consisted in being able to decide alone upon the measures to be adopted for averting the pressing danger, to do whatever he deemed proper without consultation, and to inflict punishment upon anyone without appeal. But the Dictator could do nothing to alter the form of the government, such as to diminish the powers of the Senate or the people, or to abrogate existing institutions and create new ones. So that, taking together the short period for which he held the office, and the limited powers which he possessed, and the fact that the Roman people were as yet uncorrupted, it is evident that it was impossible for him to exceed his powers and to harm the republic ; which on the contrary, as all experience shows, was always benefited by him.

And truly, of all the institutions of Rome, this one deserves to be counted amongst those to which she was most indebted for her greatness and dominion. For without some such an institution Rome would with difficulty have escaped the many extraordinary dangers that befell her ; for the customary proceedings of republics are slow, no magistrate or council being permitted to act independently, but being in almost all instances obliged to act in concert one with the other, so that often much time is required to harmonize their several opinions ; and tardy measures are most dangerous when the occasion requires prompt action. And therefore all republics should have some institution similar to the dictatorship.

The republic of Venice had reserved to a small number of citizens the power of deciding all urgent matters without referring their decisions to a larger council. And when a republic lacks some such system, a strict observance of the established laws will expose her to ruin ; or, to save her from such danger, the laws will have to be disregarded. Now in a well-ordered republic it should never be necessary to resort to extra-constitutional measures ; for although they may for the time be beneficial, yet the precedent is pernicious, for if the practice is once established of disregarding the laws for good objects, they will in a little while be disregarded under that pretext for evil purposes. Thus no republic will ever be perfect if she has not by law provided for everything, having a remedy for every emergency, and fixed rules for applying it. And therefore I will say, in conclusion, that those republics which in time of danger cannot resort to a dictatorship, or some similar authority, will generally be ruined when grave occasions occur.

CITIZENS WHO HAVE BEEN HONOURED WITH THE HIGHER OFFICES SHOULD NOT DISDAIN LESS IMPORTANT ONES

The Romans had made Marcus Fabius and C. Manilius Consuls, and had gained a most glorious victory over the Veienti and the Etruscans, which, however, cost the life of Quintus Fabius, brother of the Consul, who had himself been Consul the year before. This ought to make us reflect how well the institutions of that city were calculated to make her great, and what an error other republics commit in deviating from her system. For although the Romans were great lovers of glory, yet they did not esteem it dishonourable to obey those whom they had at a previous time commanded, or to serve in that army of which themselves had been chiefs. This custom is is entirely contrary to the opinion, rules, and practice of our times ; and in Venice they even yet hold to the error that a citizen who has once held a high post under the State would be dishonoured by accepting a lower one ; and the city consents to what she cannot change. However honourable this may be for a private citizen, yet for the public it is absolutely useless. A republic can and should have more hope and confidence in that citizen who from a superior grade descends to accept a less important one, than in him who from an inferior employment mounts to the exercise of a superior one ; for the latter cannot reasonably be relied upon unless he is surrounded by men of such respectability and virtue that his inexperience may in some measure be compensated for by their counsel and authority. If they had had the same prejudice in Rome as in Venice and the other modern states, so that a man who had once been Consul had refused to return to the army except in the quality of Consul, it would have given rise to infinite inconveniences, greatly to the prejudice of public liberty, because of the errors of the new men in office, as well as of their ambition, which they could indulge the more freely, not having any men around them in whose presence they would be afraid to commit such faults; and thus they would have been more unrestrained, which would have resulted greatly to the public detriment.

WHAT TROUBLES RESULTED IN ROME FROM THE ENACTMENT OF THE AGRARIAN LAW, AND HOW VERY WRONG IT IS TO MAKE LAWS THAT ARE RETROSPECTIVE AND CONTRARY TO OLD ESTABLISHED CUSTOMS

It was a saying of ancient writers, that men afflict themselves in evil, and become weary of the good, and that both these dispositions produce the same effects. For when men are no longer obliged to fight from necessity, they fight from ambition, which passion is so powerful in the hearts of men that it never leaves them, no matter to what height they may rise. The reason of this is that nature has created men so that they desire everything, but are unable to attain it; desire being thus always greater than the faculty of acquiring, discontent with what they have and dissatisfaction with themselves result from it. This causes the changes in their fortunes; for as some men desire to have more, whilst others fear to lose what they have, enmities and war are the consequences; and this brings about the ruin of one province and the elevation of another. I have made these remarks because the Roman people were not content with having secured themselves against the nobles by the creation of the Tribunes, to which they had been driven by necessity. Having obtained this, they soon began to fight from ambition, and wanted to divide with the nobles their honours and possessions, being those things which men value most. Thence the frenzy that occasioned the contentions about the agrarian law, which finally caused the destruction of the Roman republic.

There were two principal points in this law ; one provided that no citizen could possess more than a certain number of acres of land, and the other that all lands taken from their enemies should be divided amongst the Roman people. This affected the nobles disadvantageously in two ways ; for those who had more land than the law allowed (which was the case with the greater part of the nobles) had to be deprived of it ; and by dividing amongst the people the lands taken from the enemy, it took from the nobles the chance of enriching themselves thereby, as they had previously done. Now, as it was a powerful class that had been thus affected, and who considered resistance to this law as a defence of the public good, whenever the subject was brought up, it occasioned, as we have said, the most violent disturbances. The nobles used all patience and every means in their power to gain time and delay action upon the subject, either by calling out an army, or by getting one Tribune to oppose another who had proposed the law, or sometimes by yielding in part, or even by sending a colony to any place where lands were to be divided.

The troubles about this agrarian law continued to disturb Rome for some time, so that the Romans began to send their armies to the extreme ends of Italy, or even beyond ; after which matters were seemingly calmed down, owing to the fact that the lands taken from the enemy were at a great distance from Rome, and remote from the eyes of the people, and were situated where it was not easy to cultivate them, and consequently they were less desirable. Besides this, the Romans became less disposed to deprive their vanquished enemies of their lands, as they had done before ; and when they did so deprive any of them of their possessions, they sent colonies to occupy them ; so that from these several causes the agrarian law lay, as it were, dormant until the time of the Gracchi, who, after having revived it, wholly destroyed the Roman republic. For the power of the adversaries of the law had increased twofold in the meantime, and its revival excited such feelings of hatred between the people and the Senate, that it led to violence and bloodshed beyond all bounds or precedent.

This shows us how much more people value riches than honours ; for the Roman nobility always yielded to the people without serious difficulties in the matter of honours, but when it came to a question of property, then they resisted with so much pertinacity that the people, to satisfy their thirst for riches, resorted to extraordinary proceedings. The intentions of the Gracchi in this matter were more praiseworthy than their prudence. For to attempt to eradicate an abuse that has grown up in a republic by the enactment of retrospective laws is a most inconsiderate proceeding, and only serves to accelerate the fatal results which the abuse tends to bring about ; but by temporizing the end will either be delayed or the evil will exhaust itself before it attains that end.

FEEBLE REPUBLICS ARE IRRESOLUTE, AND KNOW NOT HOW TO TAKE A DECIDED PART ; AND WHENEVER THEY DO, IT IS MORE THE RESULT OF NECESSITY THAN OF CHOICE

The prevalence of a terrible pestilence in Rome made the Volscians and Æqueans think the moment favourable for attacking her. They therefore raised a powerful army, and assailed the Latins and Hernicians, who seeing their country ravaged felt constrained to notify the Romans, so that they might come to their defence ; but they, being afflicted by the pestilence, replied to the application of the Latins and Hernicians that they must defend themselves with their own armies, as they were not then in condition to aid them. In this we recognize the sagacity as well as the generosity of the Roman Senate, who, although it was their policy under all circumstances to remain the chief source for directing the resolves and actions of their subjects, yet they were never ashamed when necessity obliged them to adopt a course different from their usual custom, or at variance with previous resolutions. I say this because on other occasions the same Senate had forbidden those same people to arm and defend themselves ; so that to a less sagacious Senate it would have seemed a lowering of their dignity now to concede to these people the privilege of their own defence. But this Senate always judged things as they ought to be judged, and always took the least objectionable course as the best. They well knew the evil of not being able to defend their subjects, and of allowing them to arm and defend themselves without the assistance of the Romans, for the reason given, and for many others that are easily understood ; nevertheless, knowing that the Latins and Hernicians would have armed themselves anyhow from necessity, the enemy being upon them, they took the honourable course, and decided that what these people would have been obliged to do anyhow should be done with their sanction ; so that, having once disobeyed from necessity, they might not accustom themselves to disobeying from choice.

And although this would seem the proper course for every republic to have pursued under the circumstances, yet feeble and ill-advised republics would never have known how to do it, nor how to gain honour to themselves from an occasion of necessity. The Duke Valentino had taken Faenza, and forced Bologna to submit to his terms ; wishing after that to return to Rome by way of Tuscany, he sent a messenger to Florence to ask permission for the passage of himself and his army through their territory. The authorities of Florence held a consultation as to what they should do under the circumstances, but no one advised granting the permission ; in which respect they did not follow the Roman policy. For as the Duke had a very strong army, and the Florentines being almost without troops, so that they could not have prevented him from passing it would have been much more to their credit and honour if the Duke had passed with their permission rather than by force ; as it was, they had nothing but shame, which would have been greatly less if they had acted differently.

Irresolute republics never take a wise course except by force ; for their weakness never allows them to resolve upon anything where there is a doubt ; and if that doubt is not overcome by some force, they remain forever in a state of suspense.

A REPUBLIC OR A PRINCE MUST FEIGN TO DO OF LIBERALITY THAT TO WHICH NECESSITY COMPELS

Prudent men make the best of circumstances in their actions, and, although constrained by necessity to a certain course, make it appear as if done from their own liberality. This discretion was wisely used by the Roman Senate when they resolved to pay the soldiery out of the public treasury, who before had been obliged to maintain themselves. But as the Senate perceived that war could not be carried on for a length of time in this manner, as they could neither lay siege to places nor move armies to a distance, and judging it necessary to be able to do both, they resolved to pay them from the public funds ; yet they did it in such a manner as to gain credit for that to which necessity compelled them ; and this favour was so acceptable to the populace that Rome was wild with joy, thinking it a great benefit, which they had never expected and would not have sought themselves. And although the Tribunes endeavoured to expose this delusion, showing that it made the burden of the people heavier instead of easier, still they could not prevent its acceptance by the people. This burden was further increased by the manner in which the Senate levied the taxes, imposing the heaviest and largest upon the nobility, and requiring them to pay first of all.

HOW BY THE DELUSIONS OF SEEMING GOOD THE PEOPLE ARE OFTEN MISLED TO DESIRE THEIR OWN RUIN ; AND HOW THEY ARE FREQUENTLY INFLUENCED BY GREAT HOPES AND BRAVE PROMISES

After the capture of the city of the Veienti, the Roman people became possessed of the idea that it would be advantageous for the city of Rome if one half of its inhabitants were to go and settle at Veii ; arguing that, inasmuch as that city was rich in lands and houses and near to Rome, one-half of the Roman citizens might thus enrich themselves without in any any way disturbing by their proximity the public affairs of

Rome. This project seemed to the Senate and the most sagacious men of Rome useless, and fraught with danger, so much so that they declared openly that they would rather suffer death than give their consent. When the subject came to be discussed, the people became so much excited against the Senate that it would have led to violence and bloodshed, had not the Senate sheltered itself behind some of the oldest and most esteemed citizens, the reverence for whom restrained the people from carrying their insolence further.

Here we have to note two things : first, that the people often, deceived by an illusory good, desire their own ruin, and, unless they are made sensible of the evil of the one and the benefit of the other course by someone in whom they have confidence, they will expose the republic to infinite peril and damage. And if it happens that the people have no confidence in anyone, as sometimes will be the case when they have been deceived before by events or men, then it will inevitably lead to the ruin of the state. Dante says upon this point in his discourse " On Monarchy," that the people often shout, " Life to our death, and death to our life ! "

If we consider now what is easy and what difficult to persuade a people to, we may make this distinction : either what you wish to persuade them to represents at first sight gain or loss, or it seems brave or cowardly. And if you propose to them anything that upon its face seems profitable and courageous, though there be really a loss concealed under it which may involve the ruin of the republic, the multitude will ever be most easily persuaded to it. But if the measure proposed seems doubtful and likely to cause loss, then it will be difficult to persuade the people to it, even though the benefit and welfare of the republic were concealed under it.

LEAGUES AND ALLIANCES WITH REPUBLICS ARE MORE TO BE TRUSTED THAN THOSE WITH PRINCES

As it is of daily occurrence that princes or republics contract leagues or friendships with each other, or that in like manner treaties and alliances are formed between a republic and a prince, it seems to me proper to examine whose faith is constant and more to be relied upon, that of a republic or that of a prince. In examining the whole subject I believe that in many instances they are equal, but that in others there is a difference ; and I believe, moreover, that agreements which are the result of force will no more be observed by a prince than by a republic, and, where either the one or the other is apprehensive of losing their state, that to save it both will break their faith and be guilty of ingratitude. Wherever fear dominates, there we shall find equal want of faith in both. Taking all things together now, I believe that in such cases which involve imminent peril there will be found somewhat more of stability in republics than in princes. For even if the republics were inspired by the same feelings and intentions as the princes, yet the fact of their movements being slower will make them take more time in forming resolutions, and therefore they will less promptly break their faith.

Alliances are broken from considerations of interest ; and in this respect republics are much more careful in the observance of treaties than princes. It would be easy to cite instances where princes for the smallest advantage have broken their faith, and where the greatest advantages have failed to induce republics to disregard theirs ; as in the case of the proposal of Themistocles to the Athenians, when in a general assembly he told them that he had something to suggest that would be of greatest advantage to their country ; but that it was of such a nature that he could not disclose it publicly without depriving them of the opportunity of availing themselves of it. The people of Athens therefore appointed Aristides as one to whom Themistocles might communicate his suggestion, upon which they would decide according to the judgment of Aristides. Themistocles thereupon showed him that the fleet of united Greece, relying upon the treaty still in force, was in such position that they, the Athenians, could easily make themselves masters of it or destroy it, which would make them arbiters of all Greece. Whereupon Aristides reported to the people that the proposed plan of Themistocles was highly advantageous but most dishonest, and therefore the people absolutely rejected it ; which would not have been done by Philip of Macedon, nor many other princes, who would only have looked to the advantages, and have gained more by their perfidy than by any other means.

MEN OFTEN DECEIVE THEMSELVES IN BELIEVING THAT BY HUMILITY THEY CAN OVERCOME INSOLENCE

We often see that humility not only is of no service, but is actually hurtful, especially when employed towards insolent men, who from jealousy or some other motive have conceived a hatred against you. Of this our historian gives proof on the occasion of the war between the Romans and Latins. For when the Samnites complained to the Romans that the Latins had attacked them, the Romans, unwilling to irritate the Latins, declined to forbid them to continue that war : this not only had the desired effect of not irritating them, but actually encouraged them to that degree that they almost immediately displayed open enmity towards the Romans. This fact shows in the clearest manner that the patience of the Romans increased the insolence of the Latins. And therefore no prince should ever forego his rank, nor should he ever voluntarily give up anything (wishing to do so honourably) unless he is able or believes himself able to hold it. For it is almost always better (matters having come to the point that he cannot give it up in the above manner) to allow it to be taken from him by force, rather than by the apprehension of force. For if he yields it from fear, it is for the purpose of avoiding war, and he will rarely escape from that ; for he to whom he has from cowardice conceded the one thing will not be satisfied, but will want to take other things from him, and his arrogance will increase as his esteem for the prince is lessened. And, on the other hand, the zeal of the prince's friends will be chilled on seeing him appear feeble or cowardly. But if, so soon as he discerns his adversary's intention, he prepares his forces, even though they be inferior, the enemy will begin to respect him, and the other neighbouring princes will appreciate him the more ; and seeing him armed for defence, those even will come to his aid who, seeing him give up himself, would never have assisted him.

This reasoning applies to the case when there is only one enemy ; but when there are several, it will always be a wise plan for the prince to yield something of his possessions to some one of them, either for the purpose of gaining him over if war has already been declared, or of detaching him from the enemies that are leagued against him.

FEEBLE STATES ARE ALWAYS UNDECIDED IN THEIR RESOLVES : AND SLOW RESOLVES ARE INVARIABLY INJURIOUS

We should observe that it is well in all deliberations to come at once to the essential point, and not always to remain in a state of indecision and uncertainty. This was evidenced in the council which the Latins held on the occasion when they contemplated detaching themselves from the Romans. For the Romans, being apprised of the evil disposition of the Latin people, wished to assure themselves upon that point, and to see whether they might regain their friendship without resorting to arms, and therefore requested the Latins to send eight of their citizens to Rome for a conference. When the Latins were informed of this, conscious of having done many things that were displeasing to the Romans, they convoked a council to decide as to who should go to Rome, and to instruct them as to what they should say. And whilst discussing the matter, their Praetor Annius said these words : " I hold it to be of highest importance for our interests that we should think rather of what we shall do than what we shall say ; when we have decided upon that, it will be easy to accommodate our words to our acts." Certainly a most correct maxim, and one that should be borne in mind by all princes and republics ; for it is impossible to explain one's self properly when in doubt and indecision as to what is to be done ; but once resolved and decided, it is easy to find suitable words. And it will always happen that in doubtful cases, where prompt resolution is required, there will be this indecision when weak men have to deliberate and resolve.

Slow and dilatory deliberations are not less injurious than indecision, especially when you have to decide in favour of an ally ; for tardiness helps no one, and generally injures yourself. It ordinarily arises from lack of courage or force, or from the evil disposition of those who have to deliberate, being influenced by passion to ruin the state or to serve some personal interests, and who therefore do not allow the deliberations to proceed, but thwart and impede them in every way. Good citizens therefore never impede deliberations, especially in matters that admit of no delay, even if they see the popular impulse tending to a dangerous course.

IT IS AN ERROR TO TAKE ADVANTAGE OF THE INTERNAL DISSENSIONS OF A CITY, AND TO ATTEMPT TO TAKE POSSESSION OF IT WHILST IN THAT CONDITION

The dissensions between the people and the nobility in the Roman republic were so great that the Veienti, together with the Tuscans, thought the opportunity favourable for crushing out the name of Rome entirely ; and having formed an army and made incursions into the Roman territory, the Senate sent Cn. Manlius and M. Fabius against them ; and when they had moved their army near to that of the Veienti, these began with insults and attacks to abuse and offend the Romans, with such a degree of temerity and insolence that it caused the Romans to forget their dissensions and to become united ; so that when it came to a regular battle between them and the Veienti and Tuscans, the Romans completely defeated and routed them. This shows how apt men are to deceive themselves in deciding upon what course they are to take, and how frequently they lose where they had confidently hoped to win. The Veienti thought that, by assailing the Romans at a moment when they were divided by internal dissensions, they would have an easy victory over them ; but their very attack restored union amongst the Romans, and that caused the defeat of the Veienti. These dissensions in republics are generally the result of idleness and peace, whilst apprehension and war are productive of union ; and therefore if the Veienti had been wise, the more they had seen the Romans divided amongst themselves, the more they would have kept war away from them, and should have tried to subjugate them by the arts of peace. The way to do this is to try and win the confidence of the citizens that are divided amongst themselves, and to manage to become the arbiter between them, unless they should have come to arms ; but having come to arms, then sparingly to favour the weaker party, so as to keep up the war and make them exhaust themselves, and not to give them occasion for the apprehension, by a display of your forces, that you intend to subjugate them and make yourself their prince. And if this course be well carried out, it will generally end in your obtaining the object you aim at.

IT MAY AT TIMES BE THE HIGHEST
WISDOM TO SIMULATE FOLLY

No one ever displayed so much sagacity, or was esteemed so wise on account of any distinguished act, as Junius Brutus in his simulation of folly. And although Titus Livius gives but one reason that induced him to this simulation, namely, that he might live in greater security and preserve his patrimony, yet if we well consider his conduct we are led to believe that he had another reason, which was that by thus avoiding observation he would have a better chance of destroying the kings, and of liberating his country, whenever an opportunity should offer.

All those who are dissatisfied with their ruler should take a lesson from this example of Brutus ; they should measure and weigh well their strength, and if sufficiently powerful to be able to declare themselves his enemies, and to make open war against the prince, then they should take that course as the least dangerous and most honourable. But if their condition be such that their forces do not suffice for open war against the prince, then they should seek by every art to win his friendship, and for this purpose employ all possible means, such as adopting his tastes, and taking delight in all things that give him pleasure. Such intimacy will ensure you tranquillity without any danger, and enable you to share the enjoyment of the prince's good fortune with him, and at the same time afford you every convenience for satisfying your resentment. True, some people say that one should not keep so close to princes as to be involved in their ruin, nor so far away but what in case of their ruin you might thereby advance your own fortunes. This middle course would undoubtedly be the best to pursue, but as I believe that impossible, one of the above-described modes must be adopted —either to go away from them entirely, or to attach yourself very closely to them ; and whoever attempts any other way, even though he be a personage of distinction, exposes himself to constant danger. Nor will it do for him to say, " I do not care for anything ; I desire neither honour nor profit ; all I want is to live quietly and without trouble "—for such excuses would not be admitted. Men of condition cannot choose their way of living, and even if they did choose it sincerely and without ambition, they would not be believed ; and were they to attempt to adhere to it, they would not be allowed to do so by others.

It is advisable then at times to feign folly, as Brutus did ; and this is sufficiently done by praising, speaking, seeing, and doing things contrary to your way of thinking, and merely to please the prince.

OF CIVIL PRINCIPALITIES [1]

Let us consider the case when a prominent citizen has become prince of his country by the favour of his fellow-citizens. This may be called a civil principality ; and to attain it requires neither great virtue nor extraordinary good fortune, but rather a happy shrewdness. I say, then, that such principalities are achieved either by the favour of the people or by that of the nobles ; for in every state there will be found two different dispositions, which result from this—that the people dislike being ruled and oppressed by the nobles, whilst the nobles seek to rule and oppress the people. And this diversity of feeling and interests engenders one of three effects in a state : these are either a principality, or a government of liberty, or licence. A principality results either from the will of the people or from that of the nobles, according as either the one or the other prevails and has the opportunity. For the nobles, seeing that they cannot resist the people, begin to have recourse to the influence and reputation of one of their own class, and make him a prince, so that under the shadow of his power they may give free scope to their desires. The people also, seeing that they cannot resist the nobles, have recourse to the influence and reputation of one man, and make him prince, so as to be protected by his authority.

[1] The Prince.

He who becomes prince by the aid of the nobles will have more difficulty in maintaining himself than he who arrives at that high station by the aid of the people. For the former finds himself surrounded by many who in their own opinion are equal to him, and for that reason he can neither command nor manage them in his own way. But he who attains the principality by favour of the people stands alone, and has around him none, or very few, that will not yield him a ready welcome. Moreover, you cannot satisfy the nobles with honesty, and without wrong to others, but it is easy to satisfy the people, whose aims are ever more honest than those of the nobles ; the latter wishing to oppress, and the former being unwilling to be oppressed. I will say further, that a prince can never assure himself of a people who are hostile to him, for they are too numerous ; the nobles on the other hand being but few, it becomes easy for a prince to make himself sure of them.

The worst that a prince may expect of a people who are unfriendly to him is that they will desert him ; but the hostile nobles he has to fear, not only lest they abandon him, but also because they will turn against him. For they, being more far-sighted and astute, always save themselves in advance, and seek to secure the favour of him who they hope may be successful. The prince also is obliged always to live with the same people ; but he can do very well without the same nobles, whom he can make and unmake at will any day, and bestow upon them or deprive them of their rank whenever it pleases him.

The better to elucidate this subject, we must consider the nobles mainly in two ways ; that is to say, they either shape their conduct so as to ally themselves entirely to your fortunes, or they do not. Those who attach themselves to you thus, if they are not rapacious, are to be honoured and loved. Those who do not attach themselves to you must be regarded in two ways. Either they are influenced by pusillanimity and a natural lack of courage, and then you may make use of them, and especially of such as are men of intelligence ; for in prosperity they will honour you, and in adversity you need not fear them. But if they purposely avoid attaching themselves to you from notions of ambition, then it is an evidence that they think more of their own interests than of yours ; and of such men a prince must beware, and look upon them as open enemies, for when adversity comes they will always turn against him and contribute to his ruin.

Anyone, therefore, who has become a prince by the favour of the people, must endeavour to preserve their goodwill, which will be easy for him, as they will ask of him no more than that he shall not oppress them. But he who, contrary to the will of the people, has become prince by the favour of the nobles, should at once and before everything else strive to win the goodwill of the people, which will be easy for him, by taking them under his protection. And as men, when they receive benefits from one of whom they expected only ill-treatment, will attach themselves readily to such a benefactor, so the people will become more kindly disposed to such a one than if he had been made prince by their favour.

A PRINCE CANNOT LIVE SECURELY IN A STATE SO LONG AS THOSE LIVE WHOM HE HAS DEPRIVED OF IT

The assassination of Tarquinius Priscus by the sons of Ancus, and the death of Servius Tullius caused by Tarquinius Superbus, prove how difficult and dangerous it is to deprive anyone of a kingdom and leave him his life, even though you try to conciliate him by benefits. We see how Tarquinius Priscus was deceived by the seemingly lawful possession of the sovereignty of Rome, which had been bestowed upon him by the people and confirmed by the Senate. He could not believe that resentment would so master the sons of Ancus that they would not be satisfied to submit to him, to whom all Rome yielded obedience. Servius Tullius in like manner deceived himself in supposing that he could win the sons of Tarquin with benefits. Thus the first may serve as a warning to all princes that they will never be safe so long as those live whom they have deprived of their possessions ; and as to the second, it should remind every potentate that old injuries can never be cancelled by new benefits, and the less so when the benefits are small in proportion to the injury inflicted.

OF CRUELTY AND CLEMENCY, AND WHETHER IT IS BETTER TO BE LOVED THAN FEARED [1]

Every prince ought to desire the reputation of being merciful, and not cruel ; at the same time, he should be careful not to misuse that mercy. Cesare Borgia was reputed cruel, yet by his cruelty he re-united the Romagna to his states, and restored that province to order, peace, and loyalty ; and if we carefully examine his course, we shall find it to have been really much more merciful than the course of the people of Florence, who, to escape the reputation of cruelty, allowed Pistoia to be destroyed. A prince, therefore, should not mind the ill repute of cruelty, when he can thereby keep his subjects united and loyal ; for a few displays of severity will really be more merciful than to allow, by an excess of clemency, disorders to occur, which are apt to result in rapine and murder ; for these injure a whole community, whilst the executions ordered by the prince fall only upon a few individuals. And, above all others, the new prince will find it almost impossible to avoid the reputation of cruelty, because new states are generally exposed to many dangers. It was on this account that Virgil made Dido to excuse the severity of her government, because it was still new.

A prince, however, should be slow to believe and to act ; nor should he be too easily alarmed by his own fears, and should proceed moderately and with prudence and humanity, so that an excess of confidence may not make him incautious, nor too much mistrust make him intolerant. This, then, gives rise to the question " whether it be better to be beloved than feared, or to be feared than beloved." It will naturally be answered that it would be desirable to be both the one and the other ; but as it is difficult to be both at the same time, it is much more safe to be feared than to be loved, when you have to choose between the two. For it may be said of men in general that they are ungrateful and fickle, dissemblers, avoiders of danger, and greedy of gain. So long as you shower benefits upon them, they are all yours ; they offer you their blood,

[1] *The Prince.*

their substance, their lives, and their children, provided the necessity for it is far off; but when it is near at hand, then they revolt. And the prince who relies upon their words, without having otherwise provided for his security, is ruined; for friendships that are won by rewards, and not by greatness and nobility of soul, although deserved, yet are not real, and cannot be depended upon in time of adversity.

Besides, men have less hesitation in offending one who makes himself beloved than one who makes himself feared; for love holds by a bond of obligation which, as mankind is bad, is broken on every occasion whenever it is for the interest of the obliged party to break it. But fear holds by the apprehension of punishment, which never leaves men. A prince, however, should make himself feared in such a manner that, if he has not won the affections of his people, he shall at least not incur their hatred; for the being feared, and not hated, can go very well together, if the prince abstains from taking the substance of his subjects, and leaves them their women. And if you should be obliged to inflict capital punishment upon anyone, then be sure to do so only when there is manifest cause and proper justification for it; and, above all things, abstain from taking people's property, for men will sooner forget the death of their fathers than the loss of their patrimony. Besides, there will never be any lack of reasons for taking people's property; and a prince who once begins to live by rapine will ever find excuses for seizing other people's property. On the other hand, reasons for taking life are not so easily found, and are more readily exhausted. But when a prince is at the head of his army, with a multitude of soldiers under his command, then it is above all things necessary for him to disregard the reputation of cruelty; for without such severity an army cannot be kept together, nor disposed for any successful feat of arms.

Amongst the many admirable qualities of Hannibal, it is related of him that, having an immense army composed of a very great variety of races of men, which he led to war in foreign countries, no quarrels ever occurred amongst them, nor were there ever any dissensions between them and their chief, either in his good or in his adverse fortunes; which can only be accounted for by his extreme cruelty. This, together with his boundless courage, made him ever venerated and terrible in the eyes of his soldiers ; and without that extreme severity all his other virtues would not have sufficed to produce that result.

Inconsiderate writers have, on the one hand, admired his great deeds, and, on the other, condemned the principal cause of the same. And the proof that his other virtues would not have sufficed him may be seen from the case of Scipio, who was one of the most remarkable men, not only of his own time, but in all history. His armies revolted in Spain solely in consequence of his extreme clemency, which allowed his soldiers more licence than comports with proper military discipline. This fact was censured in the Roman Senate by Fabius Maximus, who called Scipio the corrupter of the Roman soldiers. The tribe of the Locrians having been wantonly destroyed by one of the lieutenants of Scipio, he neither punished him for that nor for his insolence—simply because of his own easy nature ; so that, when somebody wished to excuse Scipio in the Senate, he said " that there were many men who knew better how to avoid errors themselves than to punish them in others." This easy nature of Scipio's would in time have dimmed his fame and glory if he had persevered in it under the Empire ; but living as he did under the government of the Senate, this dangerous quality of his was not only covered up, but actually redounded to his honour.

To come back now to the question whether it be better to be beloved than feared, I conclude that, as men love of their own free will, but are inspired with fear by the will of the prince, a wise prince should always rely upon himself, and not upon the will of others ; but, above all, should he always strive to avoid being hated, as I have already said above.

IN WHAT MANNER PRINCES SHOULD KEEP THEIR FAITH [1]

It must be evident to everyone that it is more praiseworthy for a prince always to maintain good faith, and practise integrity rather than craft and deceit. And yet the experience of our own times has shown that those princes have achieved great things

[1] *The Prince.*

who made small account of good faith, and who understood by cunning to circumvent the intelligence of others ; and that in the end they got the better of those whose actions were dictated by loyalty and good faith. You must know, therefore, that there are two ways of carrying on a contest ; the one by law, and the other by force. The first is practised by men, and the other by animals ; and as the first is often insufficient, it becomes necessary to resort to the second.

A prince then should know how to employ the nature of man, and that of beasts as well. This was figuratively taught by ancient writers, who relate how Achilles and many other princes were given to Chiron the centaur to be nurtured, and how they were trained under his tutorship ; which fable means nothing else than that their preceptor combined the qualities of the man and the beast ; and that a prince, to succeed, will have to employ both the one and the other nature, as the one without the other cannot produce lasting results.

It being necessary then for a prince to know well how to employ the nature of the beasts, he should be able to assume both that of the fox and that of the lion ; for whilst the latter cannot escape the traps laid for him, the former cannot defend himself against the wolves. A prince should be a fox, to know the traps and snares ; and a lion, to be able to frighten the wolves ; for those who simply hold to the nature of the lion do not understand their business.

A sagacious prince then cannot and should not fulfil his pledges when their observance is contrary to his interest, and when the causes that induced him to pledge his faith no longer exist. If men were all good, then indeed this precept would be bad ; but as men are naturally bad, and will not observe their faith towards you, you must, in the same way, not observe yours to them ; and no prince ever yet lacked legitimate reasons with which to colour his want of good faith. Innumerable modern examples could be given of this ; and it could easily be shown how many treaties of peace, and how many engagements, have been made null and void by the faithlessness of princes ; and he who has best known how to play the fox has ever been the most successful.

But it is necessary that the prince should know how to colour this nature well, and how to be a great hypocrite and dissembler.

For men are so simple, and yield so much to immediate necessity, that the deceiver will never lack dupes. I will even venture to say that to have and to practise the above-mentioned qualities constantly is pernicious, but to seem to have them is useful. For instance, a prince should seem to be merciful, faithful, humane, religious, and upright, and should even be so in reality ; but he should have his mind so trained that, when occasion requires it, he may know how to change to the opposite. And it must be understood that a prince, and especially one who has but recently acquired his state, cannot perform all those things which cause men to be esteemed as good ; he being often obliged, for the sake of maintaining his state, to act contrary to humanity, charity, and religion. And therefore is it necessary that he should have a versatile mind, capable of changing readily, according as the winds and changes of fortune bid him ; and, as has been said above, not to swerve from the good if possible, but to know how to resort to evil if necessity demands it.

A prince then should be very careful never to allow anything to escape his lips that does not abound in the above-named five qualities, so that to see and to hear him he may seem all charity, integrity, and humanity, all uprightness, and all piety. And more than all else is it necessary for a prince to seem to possess the last quality ; for mankind in general judge more by what they see and hear than by what they feel, everyone being capable of the former, and but few of the latter. Everybody sees what you seem to be, but few really feel what you are ; and these few dare not oppose the opinion of the many, who are protected by the majesty of the state ; for the actions of all men, and especially those of princes, are judged by the result, where there is no other judge to whom to appeal.

A prince then should look mainly to the successful mainten-ance of his state. The means which he employs for this will always be accounted honourable, and will be praised by everybody ; for the common people are always taken by appearances and by results, and it is the vulgar mass that constitutes the world. But a very few have rank and station, whilst the many have nothing to sustain them. A certain prince of our time, whom it is well not to name, never preached anything but peace and good faith ; but if he had always observed either the one or the other, it would in most instances have cost him his reputation or his state.

A PRINCE MUST AVOID BEING CONTEMNED AND HATED [1]

Having thus considered separately the most important of the above-mentioned qualities which a prince should possess, I will now briefly discuss the others under this general maxim : that a prince should endeavour to avoid everything that would tend to make him odious and contemned. And in proportion as he avoids that will he have performed his part well, and need fear no danger from any other vices. Above all, a prince makes himself odious by rapacity, that is, by taking away from his subjects their property and their women, from which he should carefully abstain. The great mass of men will live quietly and contentedly, provided you do not rob them of their substance and their honour ; so that you will have to contend only with the ambition of a few, which is easily restrained in various ways.

A prince becomes despised when he incurs by his acts the reputation of being variable, inconstant, effeminate, pusillanimous, and irresolute ; he should therefore guard against this as against a dangerous rock, and should strive to display in all his actions grandeur, courage, gravity, and determination. And in judging the private causes of his subjects, his decisions should be irrevocable. Thus will he maintain himself in such esteem that no one will think of deceiving or betraying him. The prince who by his habitual conduct gives cause for such an opinion of himself will acquire so great a reputation that it will be difficult to conspire against him, or to attack him ; provided that it be generally known that he is truly excellent, and revered by his subjects. For there are two things which a prince has to fear : the one, attempts against him by his own subjects ; and the other, attacks from without by powerful foreigners. Against the latter he will be able to defend himself by good armies and good allies, and whoever has the one will not lack the other. And so long as his external affairs are kept quiet, his internal security will not be disturbed, unless it should

[1] *The Prince.*

be by a conspiracy. And even if he were to be assailed from without, if he has a well-organized army and has lived as he should have done, he will always (unless he should give way himself) be able to withstand any such attacks. But even when at peace externally, it nevertheless behoves the prince to be on his guard, lest his subjects conspire against him secretly. He will however, be sufficiently secure against this, if he avoids being hated and despised, and keeps his subjects well satisfied with himself, which should ever be his aim, as I have already explained above. Not to be hated nor contemned by the mass of the people is one of the best safeguards for a prince against conspiracies ; for conspirators always believe that the death of the prince will be satisfactory to the people ; but when they know that it will rather offend than conciliate the people, they will not venture upon such a course, for the difficulties that surround conspirators are infinite.

HOW PRINCES SHOULD CONDUCT THEMSELVES TO ACQUIRE A REPUTATION [1]

Nothing makes a prince so much esteemed as the undertaking of great enterprises and the setting a noble example in his own person. A prince, furthermore, becomes esteemed when he shows himself either a true friend or a real enemy ; that is, when, regardless of consequences, he declares himself openly for or against another, which will always be more creditable to him than to remain neutral. For if two of your neighbouring potentates should come to war amongst themselves, they are either of such character that, when either of them has been defeated, you will have cause to fear the conqueror or not. In either case, it will always be better for you to declare yourself openly and make fair war ; for if you fail to do so, you will be very apt to fall a prey to the victor, to the delight and satisfaction of the defeated party, and you will have no claim for protection or assistance from either the one or the other. For the conqueror will want no doubtful friends, who did not stand by him in time of trial ; and the defeated party will not forgive you for having refused, with arms in hand, to take the chance of his fortunes.

[1] *The Prince.*

When Antiochus came into Greece, having been sent by the Aetolians to drive out the Romans, he sent ambassadors to the Achaeans, who were friends of the Romans, to induce them to remain neutral ; whilst the Romans, on the other hand, urged them to take up arms in their behalf. When the matter came up for deliberation in the council of the Achaeans, and the ambassadors of Antiochus endeavoured to persuade them to remain neutral, the Roman legate replied : "As to the course which is said to be the best and most advantageous for your State, not to intervene in our war, I can assure you that the very reverse will be the case ; for by not intervening you will, without thanks and without credit, remain a prize to the victor."

And it will always be the case that he who is not your friend will claim neutrality at your hands, whilst your friend will ask your armed intervention in his favour. Irresolute princes, for the sake of avoiding immediate danger, adopt most frequently the course of neutrality, and are generally ruined in consequence. But when a prince declares himself boldly in favour of one party, and that party proves victorious, even though the victor be powerful, and you are at his discretion, yet he is bound to you in love and obligation ; and men are never so base as to repay these by such flagrant ingratitude as the oppressing you under these circumstances would be.

Moreover, victories are never so complete as to dispense the victor from all regard for justice. But when the party whom you have supported loses, then he will ever after receive you as a friend, and, when able, will assist you in turn ; and thus you will have become the sharer of a fortune which in time may be retrieved.

In the second case, when the contending parties are such that you need not fear the victor, then it is the more prudent to give him your support ; for you thereby aid one to ruin the other, whom he should save if he were wise ; for although he has defeated his adversary, yet he remains at your discretion, inasmuch as without your assistance victory would have been impossible for him. And here it should be noted, that a prince ought carefully to avoid making common cause with anyone more powerful than himself, for the purpose of attacking another power, unless he should be compelled to do so by necessity. For if the former is victorious, then you are at his mercy ; and princes should, if possible, avoid placing themselves in such a position.

Nor is it to be supposed that a state can ever adopt a course that is entirely safe ; on the contrary, a prince must make up his mind to take the chance of all the doubts and uncertainties ; for such is the order of things that one inconvenience cannot be avoided except at the risk of being exposed to another. And it is the province of prudence to discriminate amongst these inconveniences, and to accept the least evil for good.

A prince should always show himself a lover of virtue, and should honour all who excel in any one of the arts, and should encourage his citizens quietly to pursue their vocations, whether of commerce, agriculture, or any other human industry ; so that the one may not abstain from embellishing his possessions for fear of their being taken from him, nor the other from opening new sources of commerce for fear of taxes. But the prince should provide rewards for those who are willing to do these things, and for all who strive to enlarge his city or state.

OF THE MINISTERS OF PRINCES [1]

The choice of his ministers is of no slight importance to a prince ; they are either good or not, according as the prince himself is sagacious or otherwise ; and upon the character of the persons with whom a prince surrounds himself depends the first impression that is formed of his own ability. If his ministers and counsellors are competent and faithful, he will be reputed wise, because he had known how to discern their capacity and how to secure their fidelity ; but if they prove otherwise, then the opinion formed of the prince will not be favourable, because of his want of judgment in their first selection.

There are three sorts of intellect : the one understands things by its own quickness of perception ; another understands them when explained by someone else ; and the third understands them neither by itself nor by the explanation of others. The first is the best, the second very good, and the third useless.

[1] *The Prince.*

The true way for a prince to know his minister is as follows ; it never fails. Whenever he sees that the minister thinks more of himself than of the prince, and that in all his doings he seeks his own advantage more than that of the State, then the prince may be sure that that man will never be a good minister, and is not to be trusted. For a man who has the administration of a state in his hands should never think of himself, but only of the prince, and should never bring anything to his notice that does not relate to the interest of the government.

On the other hand, the prince, by way of securing the devotion of his minister, should think of him and bind him to himself by obligations ; he should bestow riches upon him, and should share the honours as well as the cares with him, and that the abundance of honours and riches conferred by the prince upon his minister may cause the latter not to desire either the one or the other from any other source, and that the weight of cares may make him dread a change, knowing that without the prince he could not sustain it. And when the relations between the prince and his minister are thus constituted, they will be able to confide in each other ; but if they be otherwise, then one or the other of them will surely come to a bad end.

HOW TO AVOID FLATTERERS [1]

I will not leave unnoticed an important subject, and an evil against which princes have much difficulty in defending themselves, if they are not extremely prudent, or have not made good choice of ministers ; and this relates to flatterers, who abound in all courts. Men are generally so well pleased with themselves and their own acts, and delude themselves to such a degree, that it is with difficulty they escape from the pest of flatterers ; and in their efforts to avoid them they expose themselves to the risk of being contemned. There is no other way of guarding against adulation, than to make people understand that they will not offend you by speaking the truth. On the other hand, when everyone feels at liberty to tell you the truth, they will be apt to be lacking in respect to you. A prudent prince there-

[1] *The Prince.*

fore should follow a middle course, choosing for ministers of his government only wise men, and to these only should he give full power to tell him the truth, and they should only be allowed to speak to him of those things which he asks of them, and of none other. But then the prince should ask them about everything, and should listen to their opinions and reflect upon them, and afterwards form his own resolutions. And he should bear himself towards all his advisers in such manner that each may know that the more freely he speaks, the more acceptable will he be. But outside of these he should not listen to anyone, but follow the course agreed upon, and be firm in his resolves. Whoever acts otherwise will either be misled by his flatterers, or will vacillate in his decisions, because of the variety of opinions ; and this will naturally result in his losing in public estimation.

A prince should always take counsel, but only when he wants it, and not when others wish to thrust it upon him ; in fact, he should rather discourage persons from tendering him advice unsolicited by him. But he should be an extensive questioner, and a patient listener to the truth respecting the things inquired about, and should even show his anger in case anyone should, for some reason, not tell him the truth.

Those who imagine that a prince who has the reputation for sagacity is not indebted for it to his own natural gifts, but to the good counsels of those who surround him, certainly deceive themselves. For it may be taken as a general and infallible rule, that a prince who is not naturally wise cannot be well advised ; unless he should perchance place himself entirely in the hands of one man, who should guide him in all things, and who would have to be a man of uncommon ability. In such a case a prince might be well directed, but it would probably not last long, because his counsellor would in a short time deprive him of his state. But a prince who is not wise himself, and takes counsel with more than one person, will never have united counsels ; for he will himself lack the ability to harmonize and combine the various counsels and suggestions. His advisers will only think of their own advantage, which the prince will neither know how to discern nor how to correct.

And things cannot well be otherwise, for men will always naturally prove bad, unless some necessity constrains them to be good. Whence we conclude that good counsels, no matter whence they may come, result wholly from the prince's own sagacity ; but the wisdom of the prince never results from good counsels.

OF THE DANGER OF BEING PROMINENT IN COUNSELLING ANY ENTERPRISE, AND HOW THAT DANGER INCREASES WITH THE IMPORTANCE OF SUCH ENTERPRISE

It is too lengthy and important a matter to attempt here to discuss the danger of becoming the chief promoter of any new enterprise that affects the interests of the many, and the difficulties of directing and bringing it to a successful conclusion, and then to maintain it. Leaving such a discussion, therefore, till a more convenient occasion, I shall speak here only of those dangers to which those expose themselves who counsel a republic or a prince to undertake some grave and important enterprise in such a manner as to take upon themselves all the responsibility of the same. For as men only judge of matters by the result, all the blame of failure is charged upon him who first advised it ; whilst in case of success he receives commendations, but the reward never equals the punishment. History relates many instances of citizens having been sent into exile for having counselled enterprises that terminated unsuccessfully. Some Roman citizens were foremost in urging the selection of Consuls from amongst the people. It happened that the first one so chosen was defeated with his army in the field, and the originators of that system would certainly have been punished if the party to conciliate which it was adopted had not been so powerful. Certainly those who counsel princes and republics are placed between two dangers. If they do not advise what seems to them for the good of the republic or the prince, regardless of the consequences to themselves, then they fail in their duty ; and if they do advise it, then it is at the risk of their position and their lives ; for all men are blind in that they judge of good or evil counsels only by the result.

In reflecting as to the means for avoiding this dilemma of either disgrace or danger, I see no other course than to take things moderately, and not to undertake to advocate any enterprize with too much zeal; but to give one's advice calmly and modestly. If then either the republic or the prince decides to follow it, they may do so, as it were, of their own will, and not as though they were drawn into it by your importunity. In adopting this course it is not reasonable to suppose that either prince or republic will manifest any ill-will towards you on account of a resolution not taken contrary to the wishes of the many. For the danger arises when your advice has caused the many to be contravened. In that case, when the result is unfortunate, they all concur in your destruction. And although by following the course which I advise you may fail to obtain that glory which is acquired by having been one against many in counselling an enterprise which success has justified, yet this is compensated for by two advantages. The first is, that you avoid all danger; and the second consists in the great credit which you will have if, after having modestly advised a certain course, your counsel is rejected, and the adoption of a different course results unfortunately. And although you cannot enjoy the glory acquired by the misfortunes of your republic or your prince, yet it must be held to be of some account.

I do not believe that I can give better advice upon this point than the above ; for to advise men to be silent and to withhold the expression of any opinion would render them useless to a republic, as well as to a prince, without avoiding danger. For after a while they would become suspect, and might even experience the same fate as that which befell a certain friend of King Perseus of Macedon. This king having been defeated by Paulus Aemilius, and having fled with a few adherents, it happened that, in discussing the late events, one of them began to point out to Perseus the many errors he had committed, to which he ascribed his ruin. "Traitor," exclaimed the king, in turning upon him, "you have waited until now to tell me all this, when there is no longer any time to remedy it"—and with these words he slew him with his own hands. Thus was this man punished for having been silent when he should have spoken, and for having spoken when he should have been silent : his having withheld his counsel from the king did not save him from danger. I believe, therefore, that it is best to adopt the course I have advised above.

ON THE INFLUENCE OF FORTUNE IN HUMAN AFFAIRS, AND HOW IT MAY BE COUNTERACTED [1]

I am well aware that many have held and still hold the opinion, that the affairs of this world are so controlled by Fortune and by the Divine Power that human wisdom and foresight cannot modify them ; that, in fact, there is no remedy against the decrees of fate, and that therefore it is not worth while to make any effort, but to yield unconditionally to the power of Fortune. This opinion has been generally accepted in our times, because of the great changes that have taken place, and are still being witnessed every day, and are beyond all human conjecture.

In reflecting upon this at times, I am myself in some measure inclined to that belief ; nevertheless, as our free will is not entirely destroyed, I judge that it may be assumed as true that Fortune to the extent of one half is the arbiter of our actions, but that she permits us to direct the other half, or perhaps a little less, ourselves. I compare this to a swollen river, which in its fury overflows the plains, tears up the trees and buildings, and sweeps the earth from one place and deposits it in another. Everyone flies before the flood, and yields to its fury, unable to resist it ; and notwithstanding this state of things, men do not, when the river is in its ordinary condition, provide against its overflow by dikes and walls, so that when it rises it may flow either in the channel thus provided for it, or that at any rate its violence may not be entirely unchecked, nor its effects prove so injurious. It is the same with Fortune, who displays her power where there is no organized valour to resist her, and where she knows that there are no dikes or walls to control her.

These remarks I deem sufficient as regards resisting Fortune in general ; but confining myself now more to particular cases, I say that we see a prince fortunate one day, and ruined the next, without his nature or any of his qualities being changed. I believe this results mainly from the causes which have been discussed at length above ; namely, that the prince who relies entirely upon fortune will be ruined according as fortune varies. I believe, further, that the prince who conforms his conduct to

[1] *The Prince.*

the spirit of the times will be fortunate ; and in the same way will he be unfortunate, if in his actions he disregards the spirit of the times. For we see men proceed in various ways to attain the end they aim at, such as glory and riches ; the one with circumspection, the other with rashness ; one with violence, another with cunning ; one with patience, and another with impetuosity ; and all may succeed in their different ways. We also see that, of two men equally prudent, the one will accomplish his designs, whilst the other fails ; and in the same way we see two men succeed equally well by two entirely different methods, the one being prudent and the other rash ; which is due to nothing else than the character of the times, to which they either conform in their proceedings or not. Whence it comes, as I have said, that two men by entirely different modes of action will achieve the same results ; whilst of two others, proceeding precisely in the same way, the one will accomplish his end, and the other not. This also causes the difference of success ; for if one man, acting with caution and patience, is also favoured by time and circumstances, he will be successful ; but if these change, then will he be ruined, unless, indeed, he changes his conduct accordingly. Nor is there any man so sagacious that he will always know how to conform to such changes of times and circumstances ; for men do not readily deviate from the course to which their nature inclines them ; and, moreover, if they have generally been prosperous by following one course, they cannot persuade themselves that it would be well to depart from it. Thus the cautious man, when the moment comes for him to strike a bold blow, will not know how to do it, and thence will he fail ; whilst, if he could have changed his nature with the times and circumstances, his usual good fortune would not have abandoned him.

I conclude, then, inasmuch as Fortune is changeable, that men who persist obstinately in their own ways will be successful only so long as those ways coincide with those of Fortune ; and whenever these differ, they fail. But, on the whole, I judge impetuosity to be better than caution ; for Fortune is a woman, and if you wish to master her, you must strike and beat her, and you will see that she allows herself to be more easily vanquished by the rash and the violent than by those who proceed more slowly and coldly. And therefore, as a woman, she ever favours

youth more than age, for youth is less cautious and more
energetic, and commands Fortune with greater audacity.

OF THE MEANS BY WHICH MEN, AND ESPECIALLY PRINCES, WIN APPLAUSE OR INCUR CENSURE [1]

I apprehend that my writing upon what manner a prince
should conduct himself towards his subjects and his allies may
be deemed presumptuous. But as my aim was to write something that might be useful to him for whom it is intended, it
has seemed to me proper to pursue the real truth of the matter,
rather than to indulge in mere speculation on the same ; for
many have imagined republics and principalities such as have
never been known to exist in reality. For the manner in which
men live is so different from the way in which they ought to
live, that he who leaves the common course for that which he
ought to follow will find that it leads him to ruin rather than to
safety. For a man who, in all respects, will carry out only his
professions of good, will be apt to be ruined amongst so many
who are evil. A prince, therefore, who desires to maintain
himself must learn to be not always good, but to be so or not
as necessity may require. Leaving aside, then, the imaginary
things concerning princes, and confining ourselves only to the
realities, I say that all men when they are spoken of, and more
especially princes, from being in a more conspicuous position,
are noted for some quality that brings them either praise or
censure. Thus one is deemed liberal, another miserly ; one man
generous, another rapacious ; one cruel, another merciful ; one
faithless, and another faithful ; one effeminate and pusillanimous,
another ferocious and brave ; one affable, another haughty ; one
lascivious, another chaste ; one sincere, the other cunning ;
one facile, another inflexible ; one grave, another frivolous ; one
religious, another sceptical ; and so on.

I am well aware that it would be most praiseworthy for a
prince to possess all of the above-named qualities that are
esteemed good ; but as he cannot have them all, nor entirely
observe them, because of his human nature, which does not
permit it, he should at least be prudent enough to know how to

[1] *The Prince.*

avoid the infamy of those vices that would rob him of his State ; and if possible also to guard against such as are likely to endanger it. But if that be not possible, then he may with less hesitation follow his natural inclinations. Nor need he care about incurring censure for such vices, without which the preservation of his State may be difficult. For, all things considered, it will be found that some things that seem like virtue will lead you to ruin if you follow them ; whilst others, that apparently are vices, will, if followed, result in your safety and well-being.

THE MIND AND CHARACTER OF MACHIAVELLI
AS REVEALED IN HIS PRIVATE LETTERS

I. LISTENING TO SAVONAROLA'S SERMONS

To Ricciardo Bechi

Florence, March 9, 1497.

IN ACCORDANCE WITH YOUR REQUEST FOR COMPLETE INFORMA-
tion as to what is going on here in the matter of the
Friar, I must tell you that after the two sermons of
which you have already received copies he preached a third
time on Carnival Sunday. After a good deal of talk he summoned all his followers to Mass to be said in St. Mark's on the
last day of Carnival and he said that at that time he would ask
the Lord to give an unmistakable sign if the things that he had
been predicting did not come of Him. And this step he took
in the intent, as some say, to draw his party together and make
it better able to defend him, since he suspected that the new
Government, which had been elected but whose composition
had not yet been announced, would be hostile to him. The
names of the new Lords were published the next day, Monday—
you have probably been minutely informed as to who they
are. The Friar, for his part, judged that more than two-thirds
of them were against him. The Pope, meantime, had sent in a
letter demanding his extradition under pain of the Interdict, and
fearing that the Government would obey the order literally,
the Friar decided, whether of his own accord or at the instance
of others, to discontinue his sermons at Santa Reparata and
withdraw to St. Mark's. The Government took office on
Thursday morning. At that time, therefore, still at Santa
Reparata, the Friar announced that in order to remove any
cause of trouble and the better to serve the glory of God, he had
decided to yield ; and he bade men to come and hear him at
St. Mark's, while women went to San Lorenzo's to hear Fra
Domenico.

So now our Friar was at home, and when you hear how boldly he began to preach there, and is continuing to preach, you will probably be not a little surprised. He was in the greatest alarm as to his own safety, believing that the new Government was resolved out of hand to destroy him. He knew, however, that many people in Florence would be involved in his ruin ; so he began with terrifying horrors, showing with arguments that must have been very effective with people not trained to thinking, that his followers were very fine people while his opponents were the worst sort of rascals. He went to any limit that seemed likely to weaken the hostile party and strengthen his own. I must tell you briefly of some of the things he said, since I was present and heard them.

The text of his first sermon at St. Mark's was Exodus i. 12 : " The more they afflicted them the more they multiplied and grew " (*Quanto magis premebant eos tanto magis multiplicabantur et crescebant*). Before coming to his explanation of the text, he declared his reasons for yielding and said : *Prudentia est recta ratio agibilium* : " Prudence is right reason in conduct." He went on to say that all men had, or had had, ends or purposes, though different ones. As for Christians, their purpose was Christ. The purposes of other men, past or present, varied or had varied according to their sects and beliefs. As we, who were Christians, applied ourselves to our purpose, which was Christ, we had to work for His glory with the greatest prudence and with the closest attention to times and circumstances. When it was time for us to risk our lives, we had to risk them. When it was time for us to go into hiding, into hiding we had to go, as Jesus and St. Paul did, according to Holy Writ. " So," he added, " we should do, and so we have done. When it was time for us to go forth and face the rage of the populace, we went forth, as we did on Ascension Day, since circumstances and the glory of God required it. Now that the glory of God requires that we give ground before wrath, we have drawn back."

After this brief argument he spoke of two hosts, one of which was warring under the banners of the Lord, and of that host was he and his followers ; and the other, which was warring under the banners of the Devil, and that was the host of his adversaries. He dwelt for some time on this theme and then finally came to the explanation of his text from Exodus. Good men, he said, grew under tribulations in two respects, in spirit and in number : in spirit, because man came into closer union with God when he battled under the command of truth ; and he became stronger through this coming closer to the source of his action, just as hot water became hotter in being brought closer to the fire, which was the source of its heat. They increased also in number, because there were three sorts of people, and, firstly, the good, " and those are they who follow me " ; and secondly, the wicked and the obstinate, and they were the Friar's antagonists. There was a third sort of people, free-living people, devoted to the quest for pleasure, people who were neither obstinate in evil nor steadfast in righteousness, since they really did not know the difference between good and evil. However, some visible contrast between the good and the evil was always coming to the fore, *quia opposita juxta se posita magis elucescunt*—oppositeness becoming more manifest through the juxtaposition of opposites. The third sort of people, therefore, came to recognize the wickedness of the wicked and the righteousness of the righteous, and they drew nigh unto the latter and aloof from the former, since everybody was naturally inclined to shun evil and follow the good. That was why the wicked languished under adversities while the good multiplied, and therefore " the more they afflicted them, *etc*." (I am putting this all very briefly, because there would hardly be room for more in the space of a letter.)

Then he went on and talked of a number of different subjects as he usually does, but all tending to discredit his enemies and prepare the ground for his next sermon. Our quarrellings, he said, might well bring upon us a tyrant who would cast down our houses and lay waste our lands ; and this was not against what he had said about a tyrant who would bring blessings to Florence and become lord of all Italy, because this latter would be driven out before very long. And with that, more or less, he ended the sermon.

The next forenoon he went on with his exposition of Exodus. Coming to the place (Ex. ii. 12) where it says that Moses " slew an Egyptian " he explained that the " Egyptian " meant wicked men in general, and " Moses " the preacher who " slew " them by calling public attention to their sins ; and he said : " O you Egyptian, now I am going to give you the full length of a knife ! " And he began to tear into books that you, my reverend sirs, had written—and the mash he made of you a dog would have refused to eat. And then he said—and this was what he had all along been coming to—that he was going to give the Egyptian another stab and a lusty one ; and he said that God had told him that there was someone in Florence who was trying to become a tyrant and was intriguing and doing one thing or another to that end ; and he went on to explain that trying to banish the Friar, to excommunicate the Friar, to prosecute the Friar, was wholly and exactly the same as trying to become a tyrant. Whereas, he said, the laws ought to be observed. He said so much that people in Florence in their guesses made public allusion to a man who is about as close to a tyrant as you are to heaven.

Later on, however, the Government wrote to the Pope in the Friar's favour, and the Friar could see that he had nothing more to fear from his enemies in Florence. At first he tried to hold his party together by vituperating his antagonists and fighting them by calling them tyrants. Now he sees that he no longer needs to do this and is changing tactics. Still urging his followers to stand together as at first, he has stopped talking of tyrants and their wickedness and is trying to rouse everybody against the Pope ; and in turning his fire upon the Pontiff he is saying of him things you might say of the worst rascal you can think of. So, as I see it, he goes on taking advantage of the moment and adapting his slanders to circumstances.

As to what people are saying of all this, as to what hopes or fears it gives them, I will leave it to you, in your wisdom, to judge. Your judgment indeed would be worth more than mine ; for you are well aware of our temperaments here, of the nature of the times we are living in, and, since you are there, of the attitude of His Holiness. I ask only one favour of you. If you have not found it very troublesome to read this letter, you will probably not find it troublesome to send me an answer, giving me your judgment as to the drift of said times and opinions as regards our affairs. *Valete*.

NICCOLÒ, Son of Messer Bernardo Machiavegli.

II. THE BIRTH OF A BABY

Marietta Corsini to Her Esteemed Husband, Nicholò, Son of Messer Machiavelli in Rome

In the name of God, December 24, 1503.

My dearest Nicholò.—You keep teasing me, but you have no reason to, for there would be more to me if you were here. Such talk from you ! You know perfectly well how happy I am when you are not here, and all the more so now when I hear that the plague is so bad where you are ! In fact, just imagine how happy I am ! On edge day and night ! That is the sort of happiness the baby is bringing me. Anyway, it would be nice if you wrote me a little more often than you do —three letters so far ! You should not take it in bad part if I have not written myself. I couldn't, having been down with fever all this time. It wasn't that I was cross. For the moment the baby is doing nicely. He looks like you : skin white as snow and a head like black velvet, and hairy all over, the way you are ! Since he is so like you I suppose I must call him handsome. By his looks you would say he was a year old. He had his eyes open before he was born and began turning the house upside down at once. As for the other one, the girl, she is not doing so very well. Please don't forget to come home ! This is all for the moment. God be with you and keep you. I am sending you a coat, two shirts, two handkerchiefs and a towel, for there is a plenty of such things here.

Your

MARIETTA, from Florence.

III. ON INDIVIDUALITY AND POLICY [1]

To Piero Soderini in Ragusa

[Undated.]

A letter of yours reached me in scarf and muffler [i.e. anonymously and during the January cold snap], but by the time I had read ten words I knew it was from you. I believe the frequency of Piombino in order to know you [I see the person from Piombino frequently and he keeps me informed as to what you are doing]. Of your difficulties and Filippo's [Strozzi's] I am certain, for one of you is suffering from too little light and the other from too much [That the negotiations you refer to came to nothing I can readily understand, since one of your agents was an idiot and the other a rascal]. January does not worry me so long as February stands erect in my hands [The failure of the negotiations last month does not seem to me important, in view of our prospects of success in those now in hand]. I am pained at Filippo's suspicions, and, holding off, await the outcome [I am surprised that Filippo does not trust So-and-So. I will move carefully and see what comes of it all]. Your letter was short but I lengthened it considerably by many re-readings. I was glad to get it because it prompted me to take a step which I had been hesitating to take and from which you, in fact, dissuade me. Only this part of your letter do I find not quite to the point. [I had been hesitating to see So-and-So, but acting on the hint in your letter, I made up my

---

[1] Soderini, sometime chairman of the Florentine government, was now, in 1513, in exile in Dalmatia, whence through Machiavelli, a former opponent, and others, he was trying to return to Florence. Eventually he got as far back as Rome, to spend the rest of his life there. This cryptic letter, of which the first paragraph taken literally is unintelligible, derives originally from Soderini's files, Soderini having embellished it with notes taken from other writings of Machiavelli. It was written apparently in reply to a letter unsigned and composed in the same cryptic style which Soderini managed to get through to Machiavelli sometime in January 1513. As a precaution against its falling into improper hands the correspondence was so worded as to be clear only to the two principals. Keeping to key words and ignoring grammatical relations one may guess the general trend of the letter which, for that matter, is famous largely because of the remarks on historical theory which Machiavelli appends to the personal paragraphs.

A. L.

mind to call on him. I find your fears of him quite unjustified. That he may have said or done what you say is possible.] Whereat I should be surprised were it not that my long experience has shown me so many and such strange things that I have taught myself to be surprised at nothing and to realize that neither through my dealings with men nor from my readings about them have I come to understand anything about their conduct or their manners of procedure. I know you and the compass of your navigation [I know what you want and just how you are going about it]. Even if your course could be criticized, as it cannot, I would not condemn it, considering the harbours to which it has guided you [considering the success you have so far had] and the hopes it still offers.

Judging not by your standards, which are the standards of virtue and wisdom, but by the standards of the many, I have come to the conclusion that in judging policies we should consider the results that have been achieved through them rather than the means by which they have been executed. One same purpose can be realized by different procedures, much as one can arrive at one same point over many different roads. Many different people reach identical ends by following very different policies. Any proof that may have been lacking to this view has now been supplied by the conduct of the present Pope and the things he has accomplished.

Hannibal and Scipio were alike supreme in military skill and won countless victories ; but the former kept his army together in Italy, won the sympathy of the Italic peoples and induced them to rebel against the Romans, by resorting to cruelty, treachery and impiety ; the latter had the same success with the peoples in Spain by kindness, fidelity to his word and devoutness. If examples taken from the Romans are to be considered unconvincing, there are, from our own time, the cases of Lorenzo de' Medici, who held Florence by disarming his people, and of Giovanni Bentivoglio, who held Bologna by arming his people. Vitelli held Castello and the present Duke of Urbino held his State by dismantling all fortresses. Count Francesco [Sforza], and many others, have made sure of their power by building fortresses. The Emperor Titus thought he was destined to lose his throne on the day when he failed to do a kindness to someone. Others have seemed to think they would lose theirs on the day when they did a favour to someone. Many people succeed in their designs by weighing and measuring everything. This present Pope has no scale or gauge to his name; but, acting aimlessly and unarmed, he succeeds in doing things that he could hardly do with the best-laid plans and the most efficient weapons. Every day we see, as we have at all times seen, the men just mentioned, and countless others who might be mentioned to the same point, now acquiring realms and domains and now losing them according to the whims of chance; and winning they are praised and losing they are scorned—only on occasion, when the loss comes after a long prosperity, is the blame laid not upon the person but upon heaven or the ill will of fate.

Just why different procedures should now help and now hinder I do not know, but I would like to know; and so, more with the idea of hearing your opinion, I will go so far as to state my own. I believe that just as nature gives people different faces so she gives them different sorts of minds and temperaments. Now people act according to their temperaments and the sort of minds they have; but, on the other hand, times and circumstances vary. That man is successful, that man, in other words, attains his purposes according to expectations, whose manner of acting happens to fit in with the times and the circumstances. That man fails whose conduct is at variance with the times and the circumstances. Whence it may come about that two men will achieve the same end by opposite methods, since each of them will be fitting the circumstances that confront him, there being as many sets of circumstances as there are places and countries. But times and circumstances are ever changing in general and in particular, while men's temperaments and manners of procedure remain what they are. That is why a man will have good luck at one moment and bad at another. To be sure, if a man were so wise as to know what the times and circumstances were going to be and were further able to adapt himself to them, he would always have good fortune, or at least avoid the bad; and the saying would come true that the wise man commands the stars and the fates. Unfortunately men as wise as that do not exist, for men, in the first place, cannot see what is in front of them, and, in the second, cannot change their natures, so that Fortune is the one to rule, holding men subject to her changes.

To sustain this view of mine I choose to stop at the examples mentioned—on them, in fact, I have based it ; and I ask them loyally to support each other. A new conqueror can win prestige by cruelty, treachery and impiety in a country where humaneness, fidelity to one's word and devoutness have long since lost favour ; just as a man may gain by humaneness, fidelity to his word and devoutness in a country where cruelty, treachery and impiety have long prevailed. The taste is offended by bitter things, but it is also disgusted by too many sweets. So men weary of the good just as they are angered by evil. These are the reasons, among others, why Italy fell to Hannibal and Spain to Scipio, those two men finding times and circumstances that fitted their manner of procedure. At the particular times in question a man like Scipio would not have succeeded as well in Italy, nor a man like Hannibal as well in Spain, as they both did in their respective countries.

NICCOLÒ MACHIAVELLI.

IV. "I MUST EITHER TALK POLITICS OR BE SILENT"

*To His Magnificence, Francesco Vettori, Ambassador
to the Supreme Pontiff, in Rome*

Florence, April 9, 1513.

Magnifice Domine Orator :

> " And I that of his colour took good heed
> Exclaimed, 'How shall I follow if thou fear
> Who hast been mine accustomed strength in need ? ' "
> —Dante, *Inf.*, III, 16–18.

This last letter of yours frightened me worse than a summons to the rack. I am pained at your even dreaming that I could be offended—pained not on my own account, for I have trained myself no longer to set any great store on anything, but on yours. I beseech you to follow the example of other people, who get along in the world by shrewdness and their skill at being nuisances rather than by talent and wisdom. As to what you tell me of Totto, I am sorry since you are. Actually I attach no great importance to the matter. If it cannot be "rolled" in one way, perhaps it can in another. ["If the stone cannot be rolled, let it be turned over and over." The expression *rotolare*, "to roll," to "work" something by political intrigue, is common in Aretino also.] Here again as always I must remind you that whenever I ask anything of you, you must not cause yourself any trouble on account of it ; for if I do not succeed in getting what I want I will not suffer any great pain.

If you have tired of figuring things out and then seeing that many times they turn out far differently from the conclusions you had come to in their regard, you are quite right, for the very same has happened to me. However, if I were able to have a talk with you, I probably could not help filling your head with all sorts of air-castles. Fortune has so devised that since I cannot talk of the silk trade or the wool trade or of profit and loss I have to talk of politics. I have only one choice : either to talk of politics or to take a vow of silence.

If I could get beyond the boundaries of the Domain I too would probably call on you in Rome to find out whether the Pope is at home and to be seen. Among all the favours he has been granting, mine, unfortunately and through my own neglect, was overlooked. I shall wait till September. I hear that Cardinal Soderini is having great doings with the Pontiff. I would like to hear whether you consider it advisable that I should write him a letter asking him to recommend me to His Holiness ; or whether it would be better for you to see the Cardinal and ask him verbally to do that favour for me ; or whether it would be better to do neither the one thing nor the other. I shall look forward to some answer from you on this point.

As for the horse, the fact of your mentioning it makes me laugh. You will pay me for it when I ask you to, and not till then.

Our archbishop must be dead by this time. May the Lord keep the souls of him and his. *Valete*.

NICCOLÒ MACHIAVELLI, Erstwhile Secretary.

V. POLITICS ; THE OBJECTIVE OBSERVER

To the Same

Florence, April 25, 1513.

Magnifice orator mibi plurimum honorande: . . . In your letter of the 21st you ask my opinion as to what induced the King of Spain to make this truce with the King of France. You can see no advantage in any direction in his doing so and since, on the one hand, you consider the King a great statesman and, on the other, can only see that he has made a mistake, you are forced to conclude that some profound consideration of policy lies at the bottom of his conduct which neither you, for the moment, nor anyone else can perceive. As a matter of fact your analysis could not be more comprehensive or more penetrating, nor do I think that there is anything to say that you have not said. However, as a way of showing that I am alive and at your service I will set down such reflections as occur to me.

I am inclined to think that your hesitation is based largely on the premise that the King of Spain is a great statesman. I answer that of course there can be no doubt that that king is more or less competent ; but I, for my part, have always found him more distinguished for craftiness and good luck than for profound statesmanship. I will not bother to go over all his doings, but come straight to this last enterprise of his which he started against the King of France in Italy before the King of England showed his hand. I have always thought and I still think that in this whole business, though things have turned out well for him, Spain has been needlessly risking his whole domain—a policy that experience has proved foolish for anybody.

I say "needlessly," for events of the year previous had spoken plainly enough. The Pope had done no end of unpleasant things to France. He had attacked that king's allies and tried to provoke a rebellion in Genoa. Spain himself had given France all sorts of provocations, in sending his troops along with those of the Church to attack dependencies of France.

But, then, when the King of France came off victorious, when
he had routed the Pope and stripped him of his armies and
was in a position to drive the Pope from Rome and Spain
from Naples, he did nothing of the sort, but manifested a
desire for peace. Spain therefore had nothing to fear from
France.

There is no merit in the agrument that is made in his defence—
that he had to defend the Kingdom [of Naples]. He could see
that the King of France had no designs in that direction, since
France was worn out and had plenty of other causes for worry.
These worries he would always have, for the Pope would never
want Naples to go back to France and the latter would have to
consider the Pope and fear combinations of the other powers,
all of which was more than enough to deter him.

It might be argued that Spain was afraid that if he did not
join the Pope and make war on France the Pope, being the
quick-tempered devil he was, would join France out of spite
and make war on him, and that therefore he was more or less
obliged to do as he did. My answer would be that in the
circumstances then prevailing, France was far more likely to
combine with Spain than with the Pope, had he been in a
position to combine with either. On that basis there was less
likelihood of having to fight. Victory was more certain in
the event of fighting. Finally, at that time, France considered
himself most grievously insulted by the Pope, whereas he had
no grievance against Spain. To be quits for that insult and at
the same time do a favour to the Council party inside the Church
he was ready to desert the Pope at any moment. It seems to
me therefore that in those circumstances the King of Spain
could have either mediated a lasting peace or negotiated an
agreement that would have been very much to his advantage.
Instead he dropped all those alternatives and chose war, though
he could well fear that the loss of a battle might cost him all
his states. He actually faced that danger when he lost at
Ravenna, for on the news of that defeat he ordered Consalvo
to be sent to Naples, considering that kingdom as good as lost,
while Castile, too, was tottering under his feet. He had no
reason in the world to assume that the Swiss would do for
him what they actually did—give him revenge for his defeat,
rescue him from his plight and restore him to an even greater

prestige than before. If, therefore, you consider Spain's policy from all points of view, you will agree that the outcome indicates craftiness and good luck rather than far-sightedness and sound statesmanship on his part. When, moreover, you find an important person making one mistake as gross as that you can take it for granted that he is going to make a thousand. I shall never believe, therefore, that Spain's present move hides anything that is not apparent. I am not impressed by kings as kings, nor in such matters am I influenced by any authority that cannot show its reason. If the facts are as you state them, I am quite ready to assume that in making this truce Spain has made another blunder, having an inadequate grasp of his situation and handling it even worse.

But suppose now we drop this hypothesis of mine and adopt yours—suppose we assume, that is, that Spain has acted with depth and far-sightedness. Let us discuss his move as though it were the move of a great statesman.

It seems to me that in order to adopt such a premise and rightly find the truth of the matter, we ought to know whether the truce was made after the late pontiff's death and the election of his successor, or before. The answer we give to that question may make a considerable difference. Not knowing the answer, I will assume that the truce was made before the Pope's death. If now I were to ask you what you would have expected Spain to do in the circumstances then confronting him, you would probably answer as you do in your letter, namely, that you would expect him to come to a thoroughgoing understanding with the King of France. To hand Lombardy back would be a way of placing France under obligations to him. It would remove any reason France might have for going to war in Italy, and so make sure of him.

Now my comment would be as follows :

On careful consideration of the facts one notes that Spain made the attack on France in hopes of beating him, and evidently placing more reliance on the Pope, on England and on the Emperor than the event justified. Spain thought the Pope would supply funds in abundance. He thought that the Emperor would launch a powerful offensive in the direction of Burgundy. He thought that England, being a young man of great means and soaring ambitions, would come on in great power once he had put to sea. In the face of such a coalition, France would accept any conditions that he, Spain, would dictate whether at home or in Italy.

Not one of those expectations was realized. Spain got some money from the Pope at the beginning, but only with the greatest difficulty. The Pope, moreover, not only would not give him money. He was always intriguing against him and doing everything possible to encompass his ruin. From the Emperor all he got was a number of visits from Cardinal Gork, characterized by harsh language and bad temper. England sent a small force of soldiers who could not get along with Spain's. Navarre was occupied before France was able to take the field. Had it not been for that, Spain's two armies would have won disgrace instead of mere contempt. One of them never left the bushes around Fontarabia. The other fell back on Pampeluna and was hardly able to hold there. Spain, therefore, found himself at his wits' end in this great concourse of friends. Far from expecting anything better of them he had every reason to fear worse, for they were all working hand and glove with France and were on better and better terms with the latter from day to day. France, meantime, by a deal with the Venetians, was getting plenty of money, and he could rely on an adequate supply of men from the Swiss.

In such great uncertainty and confusion Spain could only come to terms with France on any basis possible. He was finding the expense unbearable. As I have heard on good authority—from people, that is, who have had letters from Spain—there is no money in that country nor any provision for raising any. The army consists exclusively of mercenaries and they were beginning to show signs of mutiny.

As I see things, therefore, in striking this truce, the King's idea was either to show his allies the error of their ways, and make them take greater interest in the war, once they had promised to ratify the truce ; or else to get the war out of the house for good and all and be rid of the great expense and peril it involved—if Pampeluna had cracked at some inopportune moment he would have lost Castile at the very least.

As regards affairs in Italy, Spain might be relying on his armies more than he reasonably can, though I do not imagine that he trusts the Swiss, the Pope or the Emperor any further

than he has to. He knows that in Italy all that he and the
Italians themselves can do is to make the best of things. In
my opinion, Spain avoided coming to a more definite agreement with France in the matter of handing over the Duchy
of Milan because, for one thing, he did not have the Duchy in
his actual possession ; and, for another, he did not consider
that that would be a profitable move from his own point of
view. I doubt, furthermore, whether France would have
accepted such an offer, not trusting either Spain or Spain's
armies. He would have thought the offer designed not to effect
an understanding between himself and Spain but to embroil
him with others.

From the standpoint of Spain himself I cannot see what
advantage he could gain by making peace at this time. France
was bound to become more and more influential in Italy however things turned out in Lombardy. Spain's armies might
have been sufficient to win the Duchy for France but, in order
to hold it, France would have been obliged to send in forces
of his own, and no small ones either. These forces would arouse
in Italians and in Spain himself the same suspicions that the
conquering army would have aroused in the first place. No
attention is being paid to pledges and promises these days.
Spain therefore could feel no more secure as the result of such
a peace. Meantime there would be one point of definite loss.
Spain would have been obliged to make peace with France
either with the consent of his various allies or without their
consent. There was no making it with their consent, it being
impossible to get France, the Venetians and the Emperor to
agree on anything. To make it without their consent would
have been a positive loss. Spain would have been tying up
with a king whom he would be making more powerful than
ever before and who, when the time came, would be more
mindful of old animosities than of recent favours. Meantime
he would be angering all other powers inside and outside Italy.
Spain had all along and alone been the one to rouse them against
France. To desert them now and go over to France would
have been too grievous a betrayal. This peace, therefore, made
as you suggest, he would have seen resulting in the certain
aggrandizement of the King of France, and in the certain loss
of his allies' goodwill ; and all in exchange for the very doubtful

loyalty of France. France, meantime, would be the one prop he still had left. Having made France powerful and the others angry, he would have to stand with France. Now wise men never, except in cases of dire necessity, place themselves at the mercy of anybody else.

I conclude, therefore, that it was a safer course for Spain to make a truce. With a truce he shows his allies their mistake, in a way that gives them no cause for complaint, and they also have an opportunity to ratify the truce. At the same time he gets the war out of the house and again upsets everything in Italy, where he sees that there is plenty to be done and undone and many a bone to pick. As I said above, he hopes that all the powers in Italy will adapt themselves to circumstances, and it is a safe guess that the Pope, the Emperor and the Swiss will not enjoy seeing France and the Venetians gaining ground in their neighbourhood. If the three together are not able to hold France and the Venetians, they will be anxious to have Spain in Lombardy. He thinks that with his help they will be strong enough to halt the advance of France and the Venetians and that therefore the Pope will soon be throwing himself into his arms. He can take it for granted that the Pope cannot come to an agreement with the Venetians or with his other allies in anything touching Romagna.

As a result of this truce, therefore, Spain sees that France's victory stands compromised, that he is not required to depend upon France's loyalty nor to fear desertion by his allies. The Emperor and the English will either ratify the truce or they will not. If they ratify it, it will be because they think it a good thing for everybody. If they do not ratify it, they will have to take greater interest in the war and attack France with far larger forces than they sent last year. In either case Spain will have achieved his purpose.

I therefore repeat that Spain's purpose was either to force the Emperor and England to wage a real war, or else, by using their prestige, to turn things to his advantage by other means than arms. Any other course, whether continuing the war or making peace, seemed to him dangerous, so he took a middle course from which either war or peace might eventuate.

If you have watched the policies His Catholic Majesty has followed and the gains he has made you will not be very much surprised at this truce. As you know he has achieved the position he now holds starting out with no great fortune. He has always had to make war with recently conquered domains behind him and with subjects of doubtful loyalty. Now the ways in which a newly conquered domain can be held, and wavering loyalties either secured or kept befuddled and irresolute, is to create great expectations of oneself, keeping people at all times wondering just how this or that adventure is to come out.

The King of Spain has grasped this need thoroughly and made good use of it. Hence his attacks on Africa, his partition of the Kingdom of Naples and all his other many doings, all of which he undertook without knowing how they would come out. The purpose, in the given case, was not so much this conquest or that, this victory or that, as to gain prestige before the peoples and by a maze of activities to keep them ever guessing and expectant. He has always been an energetic provider of initiatives, leaving outcomes to be determined more or less by chance or by necessities. So far he has had little reason to complain either of his luck or of his venturesome spirit.

In proof of this I will mention his partition of the Kingdom of Naples with the King of France. He must surely have realized that that policy would lead to war between him and France, though he could not have foreseen within a thousand miles what the outcome was actually to be. He could not even have dreamed that he would beat the King of France first in Apulia, then in Calabria and then on the Garigliano. He, for his part, was satisfied with just starting something in order to keep in the public eye and win prestige, hoping thereafter to get out of any predicament he might fall into, by hook or by crook. So as long as he lives he will go on from one disturbance to another, never knowing in advance how things will turn out.

All this argument has been based on the assumption that Pope Julius was still alive. But even if Spain had heard that the Pope had died and that his successor had come to the throne, I believe his conduct would have been very much the same. He could not have trusted Julius, in view of that Pope's untrustworthiness, quick temper, impulsiveness and stinginess. Spain is too intelligent a man to have any great hopes of the present Pope. If Spain, moreover, is any statesman at all, he will not be swayed by interests that have changed for the worse. At that time he was following the lead of others. Now he holds the initiative himself. At that time he was risking the property of others. Now he is risking his own. He made war in his own interests. So now, in his own interests, he is making peace. Spain must understand that His Holiness will not care, *nisi coactus*, to mix either his shekels or his armies in with Christians, and I doubt whether anybody will venture to force his hand.

I imagine you will find this letter a good deal of a jumble and you may question even its soundness. My excuse must be that I am far removed in spirit from all such matters, as is witnessed by the fact that I am in retirement in the country here, never see a human face and know nothing of what is going on in the world. I have to speculate in the dark and base my conclusions on the facts that you yourself supply. Forgive me, therefore, please, and remember me to everybody there, especially to your man Paolo, in case he has not yet started home.

Your boon companion, N. M.

VI. THE SWISS AND THE ARMED NATION

To Francesco Vettori

Florence, August 26, 1513.

My lord Ambassador.—The brilliancy of your letter of the 20th left me amazed. The way you developed it, the number of its arguments and all its other qualities so discouraged me that at first I sat altogether bewildered and stunned. Had I not regained confidence in the course of later readings I would frankly have lost my temper and refused to argue with you on this subject. On this point of greater familiarity my experience was that of the fox that saw the lion. The first time he nearly died of fright. The second time he stopped and peered out at him from behind a bush. The third time he edged up and spoke to him. So I plucked up courage as I grew more intimate with your letter and I now make bold to answer.

As for the present state of the world, I conclude that we are governed by princes who, whether by endowment of nature or for some other reason, may be described as follows : a Pope who knows his business and therefore talks circumspectly and acts cautiously ; an Emperor who is irresolute and ever changing his mind ; a King of France who is contemptuous and lacking in self-confidence ; a King of Spain who is grasping and stingy ; a King of England who is rich, cruel and ambitious for glory ; then Swiss who are brutish, insolent—and victorious ; and we Italians who are poor, vain and altogether base. If I do not mention other rulers it is because I do not happen to know them.

Taking all these traits into account in connection with things that are at present going on, I agree with the friar who said *Pax, pax ; et non erit pax* ; and I grant you that any sort of peace is difficult, the one you propose as well as the one I propose. If you insist that my scheme for peace involves the greater difficulties, I defer to your judgment ; but I ask you to listen patiently to my reasons, both those that make me doubt that you are right and those that make me certain that you are wrong.

As for the doubts, it seems to me, in the first place, that you go too fast in making out the King of France a nobody and this King of England a very important man. I can't believe that France has only ten thousand soldiers. He can get plenty from his own country even if he has no Germans—men who may not be as well trained as the Germans but who are as good, at any rate, as the English. What gives me this impression is that I see that with all his dash, all his great army, all his resolve to make a mash of everybody, the King of England has not yet taken Tarroane, which is a fort about the size of Empoli and should have fallen at the first assault, and this at a time when everybody is in a hurry. This fact alone inclines me not to be too afraid of England and not to take France too lightly.

As for the slowness of France in getting under way, I think that that is choice on his part and not fear. His idea is that if winter comes before England gets a foothold in the country, England will be obliged either to go back to his island or to hang on in France at his great peril. The terrain, I hear, is marshy and without a tree. The English must be in a bad way already. That is why I thought the Pope and Spain had no great difficulty in getting a hearing from England. In the second place, the fact that France refused to give up the idea of the Council seems to me to confirm the above opinion. If the King of France were in any great trouble he would need everybody and try to stand well with everybody.

That England has sent money to the Swiss I can well believe.
That he sent it through the Emperor would very much surprise
me. The Emperor, I should judge, would prefer to spend it
on his own men and not on the Swiss.

I cannot get it into my head how this Emperor can be so
thoughtless, and the rest of Germany so indifferent, as to allow
the Swiss to gain such great influence. When I see that such is
none the less the case I lose faith in my judgment on any subject,
since that certainly is all at variance with any rational view a man
might have of it. Nor can I see either how the Swiss could
have failed to take the castle at Milan when they might have had
it. I should have guessed that with that fortress in their hands
they would have had everything they wanted and that they
should have preferred taking it for themselves to going off and
conquering Burgundy for the Emperor.

Where I think you are entirely wrong is in the matter of the
Swiss. You wonder to what extent they are to be feared. In
my opinion they constitute a very grave danger. Casa knows,
and so do many of my friends with whom I ordinarily discuss
such matters, that I had no very high regard for the Venetians
even in the days of their greatest power. I always found it
much more strange that they should have conquered and held
their empire than that they should have lost it. Their ruin
was far too creditable to them, for what a King of France
actually did a Duke Valentine could just as well have done, or
any reputable captain coming to the fore in Italy with as many
as fifteen thousand men. What amazed me was their way of
doing things, without generals or soldiers of their own. Well,
the same considerations that inclined me not to be afraid
of the Venetians impel me to be very much afraid of the
Swiss.

I do not know just what Aristotle says about countries that
have been destroyed. What interests me more than theory is
what is, what has been, and what may reasonably happen. I
remember reading somewhere that the Lucomonians held all
Italy up to the Alps and were finally driven from Lombardy by
the Gauls. If the Aetolians and the Achaeans made no great
progress, the fault lay rather with the circumstances they
encountered than with themselves. They had a King of Mace-
donia at their backs. He was very powerful and never let them

take wing from the nest. After him came the Romans. The strength of their opponents, therefore, rather than any defect in their own organization, was responsible for their failure to expand.

Now the Swiss are unwilling to acquire subjects because they do not consider it to their interest to do so. That is what they say now, because they do not see the interest. But as I said to you in the other matter, things develop gradually and human beings often find themselves obliged of necessity to do things that they have no inclination to do. It is the habit of peoples to move slowly. As things stand at present the Swiss have a Duchy of Milan and a Pope paying tribute to them in Italy. This tribute they have come to think of as a regular income and they will not be willing to do without it. When, in course of time, one of the tributaries fails to pay they will regard the failure as rebellion. They will resort to arms to collect it and, if they win, they will make sure that no such failure occurs again. In so doing they will still further bridle people whom they have already tamed. So, little by little, the whole of Italy will be dragged in.

You say that there are forces in Italy that may some day count. Place no reliance on that. It is impossible. In the first place, the forces you mention would have several leaders all at odds with one another, and there is no apparent way of finding one leader capable of holding them all united. In the second place, there are the Swiss themselves. You must never forget this : the best armies are the armies of armed peoples. Only armies of the same sort can resist them. Think again of all the armies that have attained some fame. You will probably mention the Romans, the Spartans, the Athenians, the Aetolians, the Achaeans, the barbarian hordes from beyond the Alps. Well, you will always find that the ones that have done great things have armed their peoples the way Ninus armed the Assyrians, Cyrus the Persians, Alexander the Macedonians. I note only Hannibal and Pyhrrus as examples of leaders who did great things with mongrel armies. That success on their part was due to their extraordinary genius as leaders. It won them such great prestige that their mixed armies were filled with the same spirit and had the same sort of organization as armed peoples. Considering the victories and defeats of the King of

France, you will observe that he has won against the Italians and the Spaniards, whose armies were of the same sort as his own. But now that he has been fighting with armed peoples, such as the Swiss and the English, he has lost, and is in danger of having little more to lose. That he would come to this pass has always been foreseen by competent observers, arguing from the fact that he has no soldiers of his own and has disarmed his subjects—a thing contrary to the policies and principles of all rulers who have been regarded as great and far-sighted statesmen. That was not the fault of the old kings of France, but of Louis XII and those after him. In a word, therefore, do not rely on Italian armies in the expectation either that they will be as homogeneous as the Swiss or that, being mixed as they will be, they will be as good as the Swiss.

You say that the Swiss are divided and disunited. But do not imagine that that fact will be of any great consequence as long as the Swiss stand by their laws, as they are going to do for some time to come. There are no heads of factions in Switzerland who have any great following, nor can there be. Now leaders without followings are soon done away with and cause no serious trouble. As for the fact that the Swiss have recently executed a number of such people, it is probably a question of some few traitors, men in public office, that is, who may have tried to help the French in roundabout ways, who were found out and put to death. But that fact is of no more importance than the fact that in Italy a thief is hanged every so often.

I do not think the Swiss are going to make an Empire such as the Romans made. I do think that in view of their nearness and our dissensions and disorders, they are likely to become arbiters of the fate of Italy. That danger worries me and I would like to find some help for it. Since the King of France has not been the man to do it, I do not see who else can. I suppose I must join you in preparing to bewail the ruin and enslavement of our country. Even if the disaster does not come to-day or to-morrow, we shall probably live to see it ; and for this privilege Italy can thank Pope Julius and others who are not supplying the remedy—granting that things have not gone too far for a remedy. *Valete.*

NICCOLÒ MACHIAVELLI.

VII. "I AM LIVING ON MY FARM IN THE COUNTRY"

To Francesco Vettori

Florence, December 10, 1513.

Your Magnificence, the Ambassador.— . . . I am here at my country place. Since those last adventures of mine I have not been three weeks in Florence all told. For the most part I have been hunting thrushes, doing everything myself. Up before dawn I prepared and spread the lime and then went about with a bundle of cages till I must have looked like Getas when he came back from port with the load of Amphitryon's books. I got a minimum of two and a maximum of six birds each day. That was the story all through September. Thereafter that contemptible and ridiculous amusement came to an end to my great sorrow, and I have gone on ever since in the manner that I shall now describe.

I get up with the sun and go off to a piece of a wood I own, where I am having the trees cut. I spend a couple of hours there going over the cutting of the day before and idling about with the cutters. They are always in some quarrel, either with one another or with the neighbours. I would have no end of comical stories to tell you in regard to this piece of forest— experiences of mine, now with Frosino da Panzano, now with others, who have given me orders for wood. Frosino, in particular, sent for a number of cords without letting me know. When it came to paying he held back ten lire on the ground that I had owed him that much for four years from a round of jacks-and-aces we played one evening at Antonio Guicciardini's. I began to raise the very devil, saying that the teamster had gone for the wood without my permission, that he was therefore a thief and that I was going to gaol him. At long last Giovanni Machiavelli interposed and made peace between us. During that cold snap we had, Battista Guicciardini, Filippo Ginori, Tommaso del Bene, and a number of other town worthies, each ordered a cord. I said they all could have it and actually ordered one sent to Tommaso. The pile reached half-way to Florence because Tommaso, his wife, his maid and his boys were all there to help stack it up, and they worked as hard as

Gabburra works on Thursdays when he and his help take a hand at beating the donkey. Well, that showed me who was getting the best of this wood business, so I told the others I had no more to sell. They all got together and made a great fuss, especially Battista, who says it is just one more disaster to add to the troubles he has been having in Prato.

After my visit to my woods, I go to the spring and from the spring to a birding-grove I have. I carry a book under my cloak—either Dante or Petrarch or one of the minor poets, say Tibullus, or Ovid. I read the tale of their passions and their loves—and think of my own, lingering beside the spring, indeed, for quite a time in these preoccupations. Thence I take the road to the tavern, talking to the people I happen to meet, asking news of their towns, and listening to all sorts of stories as throwing light on the varying taste and whims of men. That takes me to dinner-time, when I meet my company and partake of such viands as befit my poor farm and my dwindling inheritance. With dinner disposed of, back to the tavern I go, and there ordinarily I find, besides the tavern-keeper, a butcher, a miller and a couple of bakers. With those idlers I idle out the livelong day, playing jacks-and-aces or trick-track. It is just one battle after another with boundless rages and personal insults. At stake most often is a farthing at the highest, but that does not prevent our shouting as loud as Saint Cassianus. So, with these lice clinging to my person, I keep my brain dusted off somewhat and provide a vent for the cruelty of my lot, satisfied that the Fates should see me humiliated in this way and hoping that perchance they may feel ashamed of themselves.

"I HAVE COMPOSED A PAMPHLET: *DE PRINCIPATIBUS*"

[From the same letter]

Evening come, I return home and go to my study, removing at the door the soiled and dusty clothes I have worn all day and gowning myself in courtly, royal induments that I may fittingly enter the lordly precincts of the men of old. There they are, welcoming me affectionately, and with them I partake of that food which alone I can call my own and to which I was born. I have the effrontery to address them and ask them their reasons for doing the things they did. They are kind souls and as a rule answer. So for four hours I am free from all annoyances, forgetting all my troubles, mastering my fears of poverty and my horror of death. I let myself be absorbed wholly in them.

Since, as Dante says, there is no knowledge apart from remembering what one has heard, I have set down some of the things that I account to profit from my intercourse with them, and so I have written a pamphlet which I am calling *De principatibus*. In it I go as deeply as I can into the subject, discussing the definition of monarchy, how many kinds of monarchies there are, and how they are won, held and lost. If you have ever liked any of my ramblings, I believe you will not dislike this one. Any head of a state, and especially a new one, should find it interesting, and therefore I am dedicating it to His Magnificence, Giuliano. Filippo Casavecchia has seen it. He can tell you more or less what it is like and also all about the talks I have had with him, though I am still expanding the text a good deal and polishing it.

I have talked with Filippo as to whether I had better offer this little book to the Medici or not, and, on the assumption that I had better do so, as to whether I should present it in person or merely send it. Not offering it, I should have to fear that Giuliano might, at the very least, read it, and that this man Ardinghelli would plume himself on being the author of this last effort of mine. To offer it I am impelled by my besetting need. I am spending my capital rapidly here, and I cannot go on in this way very long without incurring disesteem because of my poverty. Then again, I am anxious for the House of Medici to begin using me at some negotiation or other, if they are ever to begin. If I should not succeed in winning them afterwards I would always be sorry I had not given them the book. Then again, if they were to read it they would see that I was not sleeping or idling all those fifteen years that I devoted to statecraft. Anybody, it seems to me, should be glad to have the services of a man who has acquired so much experience at the expense of other employers. Of my trustworthiness there could be no doubt. Having so long kept faith with people, I would not be likely to begin betraying now. A man who has kept his word loyally for forty-three years, as I have, could not change his nature very easily. The fact that I am a poor man is proof of my loyalty and honour. . . .

I do wish you would write me your opinion on all this. Please do ! *Sis felix.*   NICCOLÒ MACHIAVEGLI.

VIII. WOMEN

To Francesco Vettori

Florence, February 4, 1514.

Your Magnificence, the Ambassador.—You say you are dismayed at the spectacle I offer as you think of all that the shafts of Love have done to me. Perhaps I ought to explain my exact policy in His regard. In two words I have let Him have His way, following His lead over hill and dale, through bush and meadow, and I find that on that basis He has treated me far better than He would have, had I tortured and tormented Him. Free Him of pack, bit and bridle, therefore, shut your eyes and say : " Go to it, Love, you be my guide and leader —if to a good end, all in your praise, if to a bad, all to your discredit ! I am your slave. You can gain nothing by torturing me—in fact, you are the loser in harming your own property." I imagine some such language as that would help, going through Him as it would through a stone wall. So then, my dear sir, live happily, be not discouraged, look Fortune in the eye, and take advantage of those opportunities which the whirling heavens, circumstance, people, lay in your way. Fear not ! You will escape every entanglement, you will surmount every obstacle. If it should occur to you to favour her with a serenade, I will hurry to your side with some fair stanza that will not fail to stir her heart.

That is about all I can think of, to send you in reply to your letter. There is nothing to report from here except prophecies and forebodings of disaster, which prophecies may God erase if they speak false, or turn to a good end, if they speak true.

Such time as I spend in Florence I divide between Donato del Corno's shop and Riccia's. I imagine I have become a good deal of a nuisance to them both. Donato says I clutter up the shop, and Riccia says I clutter up the house. In both cases I have been putting my reputation for brains to good use, and with such luck so far that Donato has kept a warm seat for me beside his fire, while Riccia lets me steal a kiss now and again on the sly. I don't imagine said luck is destined to last very long. The advice I have been giving the two has in no case panned out. In fact this very day Riccia said to me, pretending to be reporting a conversation she had had with her maid : " These great intellects ! These wiseacres ! I don't know where they keep their brains. My opinion is they all get everything upside down."

Magnificent Ambassador, you see the devilish fix I am in. I really would like to keep hold of these two people, but I don't see how I am going to. If anything should occur to you, or Filippo, or Brancaccio, I would be grateful if you would send it on. *Valete.*

NICCOLÒ MACHIAVELLI.

To Francesco Vettori

Florence, June 10, 1514.

Magnificent Ambassador.—I received your two letters in the country, where I am living with my company. Donato sent them on, on behalf of Brancaccio. I answered in the terms that seemed most appropriate, in the matter of my private affairs, your heart problems and all the rest ; but then I came on here to Florence for two days and forgot everything. I would find it some trouble to repeat all that I wrote. I will wait, therefore, and send the letter later, here just explaining briefly that I did not go to Rome for the very reasons that you now state to me. I had divined them all by myself.

So I shall continue on here among these lice of mine, without finding anybody who remembers my record in service or who thinks I am good for anything. But I can't continue very long in this way. My funds are giving out and I can see that if the Almighty does not show Himself better disposed towards me I shall some day be obliged to leave home, take a post as reader or bookkeeper to some constable, if I can't do any better, or go to some out-of-the-way place to teach children their letters, allowing the people here, meantime, to imagine that I am dead

For that matter I am quite a burden to them. I am in the habit of spending and cannot do without spending.

I am not saying all this with the idea that you are to put yourself to any trouble or inconvenience in my behalf, but just to get this wretched matter off my chest and never mention it to you again.

De amore vestro, I will remind you that Love tortures people who try to tie Him up or clip His wings when He flits into their hearts. Being a child and capricious, He digs out their eyes, their hearts and their—guts. But then there are those who like him and pamper him in his whims. When he would go, they let him go. When he would return, they welcome him back joyously.

Such are always blessed by Him with attentions and endearments and they triumph under His rule. Therefore, my dear fellow, do not try to stabilize one who is volatile by nature. Do not try to clip the wings of one who for every feather you spare Him gives you a thousand wherewith to soar on high. So will you fare well.

NICCOLÒ MACHIAVELLI.

To Francesco Vettori

Florence, August 3, 1514.

My dear friend.—Your several accounts of your love affairs in Rome have filled me with gaiety. As I read and thought of all your pleasures and pains (for the former are never so zestful without the latter), no end of burdens seemed to be lifted from my spirit. I am lucky enough, as it so happens, to be able to pay you back in your own coin. While I was in the country I came upon a creature so delightful, so gracious, so noble, both by nature and by the improvements on nature, that I could not praise her or love her so extravagantly that she would not deserve more.

I suppose that I should tell you, as you told me, how it all began, with what nets Love captured me, where He set them and what their texture. The answer would be : nets of gold, set among flowers, woven by Venus, and so sweet and so gracious that, though a boor might have torn free from them, I simply refused to. Well, I lay basking in their embrace so long that the slender strands became stout bonds, with the meshes tightly knotted. Do not imagine that in catching me in this way Love used any ordinary procedures. Knowing well that such would not have served He applied most unusual devices, which I was unable, or at least unwilling, to elude. To put it all in a word : here I am, a man of fifty, yet these dazzling suns do not blind me, this rough going does not tire me, these dark nights do not frighten me. Everything seems easy to me and I adapt myself to her every desire, even desires that normally would be different from mine or flatly contrary. I realize that I have assumed a very considerable undertaking, but I am infinitely happy with it, both because of what this rare and delightful beauty brings to me and because it takes my troubles off my mind, so that I would not part with it for anything in the world.

So I have dismissed all thought of great and serious things. I am not reading the ancients nor discoursing on the moderns. My one concern is with sweetness, for which praises be to Venus and all Cypria. If you have anything to tell me about your girl, let me have it. Your thoughts on other subjects you may communicate to those who prize them more than I do and have a better comprehension of them. Serious concerns have never brought me anything but torment, the frivolous never anything but happiness and delight. *Valete.* Yours,

NICCOLÒ MACHIAVELLI.

IX. DANGERS OF NEUTRALITY

To Francesco Vettori

December 22, 1514.

. . . I do not believe that a policy of neutrality has ever been advantageous under conditions where one is less powerful than either or any of the belligerents and has territories interspersed with theirs. You must understand that it is of supreme importance to a ruler to so steer his course with his subjects, friends and neighbours that he will not be hated or despised. If he has to incur one of the two things he should disregard the hatred but

8

studiously avoid the contempt. Pope Julius never cared whether he was hated or not, so long as he was feared and respected ; and through the fear that he inspired he turned the world upside down and brought the Church to the position she occupies to-day. I assure you that a neutral is bound to be hated by those who lose and despised by those who win. The moment people begin to ignore a ruler, and he comes to be considered useless as a friend and not dangerous as an enemy, there is every reason to foresee that every sort of insult will be offered him and every sort of intrigue plotted to his ruin. The winner will never be without pretexts. Since, on our premise, territories are closely connected, the neutral will be obliged to receive now the one belligerent, now the other, into his ports, and entertain them, and assist them with lodgings and supplies. They will all assume that they are being tricked and no end of disputes, no end of incidents, will arise. Even if a war could be conducted without such incidents, as it can never be, they will arise after the victory ; for those who are less powerful than you and afraid of you will flock to the winner's side and provide him with all manner of opportunities to detest you. If one were to say, " Yes, but if I lose that, I can keep this," I would answer that it is better to lose everything courageously than a part ignominiously, for one cannot lose the part without endangering the whole. . . .

[To the same, in answer to a second letter of the same date]

. . . Though I hear the policy of neutrality lauded on all hands, I cannot approve of it. In all my experience with public affairs and in all the history I have read, I cannot think of a case where the following of a policy of neutrality has ever been advantageous. Quite to the contrary, such policies have always been disastrous and have led straight to ruin. The reasons for this you know better than I, but I will venture to state them. You are well aware that the chief concern of any government must be to keep from being hated and despised—*fugere in effectu contemptum et odium* ; and this applies to its relations with its citizens as well as to its relations with its neighbours. As long as a government manages to do this, things will go well : but the moment it fails to avoid contempt, in particular, it is done for,

Now I believe that to follow a policy of neutrality between two peoples at war is to set out deliberately to be hated and despised. One of the belligerents will be sure to feel that in return for favours received in the past or in consideration of long-standing friendship, you ought to throw in your lot with his, and when you fail to live up to the obligation he comes to hate you. The other will despise you because he now discovers that you are cowardly and irresolute. There at one blow you have earned the reputation of being a useless friend and a negligible enemy, and whoever wins will harm you as he pleases. To this point one might quote the words that Livy puts into the mouth of Titus Flaminius in an address to the Achaeans, whom Antiochus had persuaded to adopt a policy of neutrality : " Nothing could be more foreign to your interests : without gratitude from anybody, respected by none, you will fall prey to whoever wins." As war proceeds, any number of reasons for hating you will arise. Most often the third party finds himself so situated that he can help or harm one of the two belligerents in many different ways. Once war has broken out, therefore, it will not be long before you find that the side you have chosen not to take openly you are obliged to take secretly and without credit to yourself ; and even if you do not do that, everyone will assume that you are doing it. If the neutral has such luck that no just cause of grievance is given to either belligerent in the course of a war, the cause of grievance will arise afterwards ; for all who are angry at the third party or afraid of him will go over to the side of the victor and supply him with pretexts for hating the third party and starting trouble. . . .

THE LONG VIEW AND THE SHORT

. . . [In choosing sides between two belligerents] one must consider not only their relative strength but the number of ways in which they each have a chance of winning. . . . One must consider, for instance, whether in joining one of them one makes his victory certain, or whether, even if one joins him, his victory remains doubtful. . . . If to-day the Pope joins the King of France, there will be no question of the latter's victory. . . . The Holiness of our Lord has two homes, one in Italy and the

other in France [Avignon]. If the Pope joins the King of
France, he risks one of his possessions. If he joins the enemies
of the King of France, he risks them both. If he goes against
France and France wins, he will necessarily have to share the
lot of the losers and go either to Switzerland to starve, to
Germany to die of boredom, or to Spain to be stripped clean
and sold at auction. If he joins France and is beaten, he will
still have France. He will still find himself with a roof over his
head, with a whole kingdom devoted to him and amounting
to a papacy, and with a king who, in one of a thousand ways,
by diplomacy or by war, can one day rise again. *Valete*—and
in endless reliance on your friendship.

X. ON GAIETY AND STATESMANSHIP

To Francesco Vettori

Florence, January 31, 1514.

Your Magnificence.— . . . I am sorry you are not here to
enjoy the spectacle of my ups and downs of mood ; but the
pleasure you are missing has fallen to our Donato, who is here
with the girl I mentioned to you some time ago. The two of
them have been the one haven and refuge for my bark, which
has long been tossing rudderless and without sails in one con-
tinuous storm. One less than two evenings ago I was in a
situation where I could say, as Phoebus said to Daphne : " Maid,
I beg of thee, flee not ! Not as foeman do I pursue ! Stay,
I beg thee ! The lamb flees the wolf, the stag the lion, the dove,
on fluttering wing, the hawk—but those are enemies all."
Unfortunately, just as such talk profited Phoebus no whit, so
the same pleas on my part availed nothing with the fugitive
I refer to.

I suppose, my dear fellow, that anyone looking at our letters
and observing the wide range of their subject-matter, would
imagine that we were two solemn celebrities with thoughts
ever fixed on matters of great moment and minds incapable of
harbouring any preoccupation that was without its nobility,
or its decency at least. But then, turning the page, the same

person might regard us as frivolous, trifling rakes with nothing but fatuities in our heads.

Now there are those who find such contrasts in the highest degree reprehensible. I think them points of merit, instead ; for we are imitating Nature in her variety, and in imitating her one never goes wrong. Now this variety you and I are wont to reflect in the sequences of our letters. . . .

XI. A POET'S WARNING TO ARIOSTO

To the Poet Lodovico Alamanni

Florence, December 17, 1517.

My esteemed Lodovico.— . . . During these past days I have been reading the *Orlando Furioso* of Ariosto, and, truly, it is a beautiful poem throughout and in not a few places altogether admirable. If you see him there in Rome give him my regards and tell him that my one sorrow is that, for all of his mentioning so many poets, he has left me out like a nobody, doing to me in said *Orlando* a thing that I shall be careful not to do to him in my *Ass*. . . .

XII. DOWRIES AS A BUSINESS

To Francesco Guicciardini [1]

1525 [Autumn].

My dear President.—I never think of your worship (and I think of you often indeed) without wondering what one might do to enable you to attain your wishes in a matter which I know is very close to your heart. Among the many fancies that have flitted through my mind there is one which I have decided to communicate to you, not so much by way of advice as to open for you a door through which you, better than anybody else, will be able to find your way.

Filippo Strozzi has no end of children on his hands, and he

---

[1] Statesman and author of *The History of Florence* ; head of a great Florentine family.

not only is trying to provide distinguished positions for his sons but considers it desirable to place his daughters well. His idea, as would be the idea of any sensible man, is that his eldest daughter should open the way to her younger sisters. Among other moves, he thought of a match for her with one of Giuliano Capponi's boys, with a dowry of four thousand florins. He had no luck there, because Giuliano did not like his proposition. Filippo was very much discouraged, concluding that he would never get anywhere on his own resources, unless he went around offering a dowry that would leave him in straits afterwards. So he appealed to the Pope for influence and financial aid. At the Pope's suggestion he opened negotiations with Lorenzo Ridolfi and arranged a match with a dowry of eight thousand florins, the Pope paying four and he four.

Pagolo Vettori wanted to make a creditable family alliance. Not seeing how he could ever provide an adequate dowry himself, he too appealed to the Pope, and to please him the Pope threw in two thousand ducats out of his own purse, along with his influence.

My dear President, if you were to be the one to break the ice by going in the direction mentioned, I doubtless would be one of those who would hesitate to advise you to do so ; but since the road has been opened for you by two men who, in respect of quality, merits and any other human consideration, are not your superiors, I suggest to you out of hand that boldly and with no qualms at all you do what they did.

Filippo had had 150,000 ducats from one Pope or another, but he made no bones of it in appealing to the Pope again in the emergency mentioned. You have not made 20,000 out of Popes and should therefore have all the less hesitation. Pagolo had been helped any number of times and in any number of different ways and not only with jobs but with cold cash. That did not restrain him from calling in the Pope again in a new case of need. Much less should you be timid about taking a similar step, since such consideration as you have received has been less a burden than a profit to His Holiness. I make no mention of Palla Rucellai, Bartolommeo Valori and countless others who have been aided from the Pope's purse in moments of need. Such precedents should make you bold in asking and certain of obtaining.

If I were in your place, therefore, I would proceed as follows :
I would write to your agent in Rome a letter that he could
read to the Pope. I would also write the Pope a letter to be
delivered to him by your agent. Your agent, quietly, would
have a copy of the letter and you would tell him to be sure
to get an answer. The letter should explain that you have
laboured for ten years for the Pope's honour and profit and
that you think that you have realized your hopes in both
regards, though at the cost of very serious sacrifices and dangers
to yourself ; for the which you are devoutly thankful first
to the Lord and then to His late Holiness, Pope Leo, and His
present Holiness, to whose trust in you you attribute all your
success. You will say that you are well aware that a man may
do ten things with great success and then make one failure
important enough to cancel all that has gone before. Considering, therefore, that you have so far been consistently successful,
you had rather not make the decisive mistake.

That much for a sort of introduction. Going on, I suggest
that you describe your present situation, your having no male
offspring, but four daughters, for one of whom you think it
high time to find a husband. If you cannot arrange a match
on a par with the position you have achieved, it will be, you
think, as though you had never done anything worth while.
I would go on, then, and point out that the only obstacle to
the realization of your hopes lies in the bad morals and wicked
ways of our times ; since things have come to such a pass
that when a young man is rich and well-born he thinks of
nothing except the size of the dowry, considering, indeed,
that unless the dowry is large, nay, exorbitant, it will be a
disgrace to him. As a result, you cannot see how you are going
to surmount this difficulty, since three thousand florins is the
highest figure that you could possibly reach. Four daughters,
therefore, would cost you twelve thousand, which would be
all the savings you have made by all the toil and danger
mentioned. Though you cannot go higher you are reasonable enough to admit that such dowries would be only half
the size of the dowries that gentlemen these days are demanding. As a last resort, accordingly, you have brought yourself
to doing what some of the best friends of His Holiness—
among whom you consider yourself one—have done : namely,

you appeal for help and influence to His Holiness in the firm persuasion that what he has done for others he will not be unwilling to do for you.

At this point I would reveal the name of the young man you have in view, going back to the point that the dowry and nothing else stands in the way. His Holiness, therefore, has to surmount this difficulty for you—and here go after him mercilessly with the strongest language you can find : your words should show the extreme importance you attach to the matter.

I am quite persuaded that if you handle this business in Rome the way it can be handled you are certain to succeed. At any rate, do not fail to do yourself justice. If time and circumstances permit, I would urge you to send your man Girolamo to Rome on this errand, for everything depends on making the request boldly and on showing that you are going to be in a very bad humour if it is not granted. Our princes are readily inclined to do new favours to people whom they have already favoured. They are so afraid of losing credit for the old favours if they refuse the new that they hasten to do the new when the new are asked in the tone of voice that I want you to use in Rome on this occasion. You understand ! . . .

To Francesco Guicciardini

Florence, December 19, 1525.

Dear President.—I have postponed answering your last letter till to-day because I did not think you regarded it as very important and because I have not been very much in Florence. Now, however, I have heard that your hostler is in town and seeing in him a guarantee of safe delivery I have decided to wait no longer.

I cannot deny that the doubts you entertain as to the wisdom of venturing on the step mentioned in the way mentioned are sound and well considered. Nevertheless I will express to you a feeling I have, that one can go wrong by being too retiring as well as by being too up-and-doing—audacity in many cases is the best. Certainly if Filippo and Pagolo had been as bashful as you are, they would not have got what they wanted to get. If Pagolo has no girls left to set a precedent for the others, Filippo has ; but he did not think of them so long as he could settle the first in the way he wanted. I do not know how much truth there may be in what you say about putting one of your girls in Paradise only to put the others in Hell ; but even if that were so you would be no worse off with the others than you are with them all now as things stand. I think you would be better off, for your other sons-in-law, in addition to counting on you could count on a distinguished brother-in-law, and you could hunt out some who would be less greedy and more honourable. Even if you did not find such, you would still have a chance to do for the other girls what you would be doing for this one. In any case I would make a try at the Pope. If I did not come to grips with him at the first onset, I would talk to him in indirect terms, bring him to understand my needs in general, hint to him that he could help me, see where he stands, advancing and drawing back according to his attitude. I must remind you of the advice the pilgrim in the story gave to the Duke of Provence, who had four daughters to find husbands for. He told him to marry the first one well, since the first would establish the rank and status of the others. The Duke went out and married the first to the King of France, giving him half of Provence for a dowry. That enabled him to marry the other three to kings with hardly any dowry at all. The story is in Dante. . . . Yours . . .

XIII. ON A MULE THAT LOST ITS MIND

To Guido, son of Niccolò Machiavelli

Imola, April 2, 1527.

Guido, my dearest boy.—I have received your letter and it was a great joy to me, especially because it told me that you are well again. No news could have made me happier. If the Lord vouchsafes life to you, and to me as well, I believe I can make something of you, especially if you do all that you ought. In addition to the important people who have been friends with me all along, I have now made friends with Cardinal Cibo—so great a friendship, indeed, that I am quite astonished. This connection will stand you in good stead. But you have got to educate yourself. Since you have no further excuse for doing wrong, work hard, learn your literature and your music. You see all the consideration that comes to me from the little talent I have. So, my boy, if you would make me happy, be successful and a credit to yourself, study hard, behave yourself, and learn. Help yourself and everybody will help you.

You say the little mule has gone crazy. Well, we have to treat him just the reverse of ordinary lunatics. Them you tie up. The little mule you must untie. So give him to Vangelo and tell Vangelo to take him to Montepugliano, and there remove his bridle and halter, and turn him loose, so that he can go where he wishes, earn his own living, and get over his craziness. There are big fields there. He is just a little mule. He can't possibly do any harm to anybody. Then, without worrying about him, we can see how he gets along. We can attend to catching him again when we are sure he has got his mind back.

Do with the other horses as Lodovico told you to do. I am glad he is well again and has sold the horses. I am sure that he has done well, since they were costing us money. But I am pained and angry that he has neglected to write.

Give my love to your mother, Marietta, and tell her that I have been on the point of leaving here from day to day, and so I am still. I have never been so eager to get back to Florence as I am now. Unfortunately I can do nothing about it. Just tell her that she must be of good cheer whatever she may hear. I will be at home before anything serious happens.

A kiss to Baccina, to Piero and to Totto, if Totto is still there. I wish you had told me how his eyes are doing. So, be cheerful, all of you, and spend as little as you can. Tell Bernardo to be careful to behave himself. Here I have written him twice in two weeks, and no answer ! The Lord keep you all.

XIV. "I LOVE MY COUNTRY MORE THAN MY SOUL"

To Francesco Vettori

Ferli, April 16, 1527.

Your Magnificence.—Monsignor della Motta went to the Imperial camp to-day with the text of the agreement that had been established in Rome. If Bourbon wants to accept the agreement he will halt his army. If he advances, it will be a sign of his refusal. In other words, to-morrow will decide what our lot is to be.

Here, in Florence, therefore, we have decided that if he advances, we will think of war and nothing else, giving not one shred of attention to talk of peace. If he halts, we will consider peace and lay aside every thought of war. With this wind that is blowing, you too must mind the tiller. If the decision is war, you must break off all paltering with peace, so that the Allies will dash forward, head down. Here there must be no limping and hopping. We must rush madly in, for despair often finds devices that cold choice has failed to find. The Imperial troops are advancing without artillery and over rough ground. If, therefore, we can combine the little life we have left with the forces of the League, which are in good shape, the Imperial army will either retire from that territory in confusion or else come to a more reasonable frame of mind. I love Francesco Guicciardini, but I love my country more than my very soul. I can tell you this, with sixty years of experience behind me : we have never been in a more ticklish situation than this one, where peace is necessary but war cannot be avoided, and where we are called upon to deal with a prince who, doing his utmost, can contribute either to peace alone or to war alone. Do not forget me.

NICCOLÒ MACHIAVELLI.

XV. "FATHER LEFT US IN DIREST POVERTY"

Piero Machiavelli to Francesco Nello

Pisa, June 22, 1527.

My dearest Francesco.—I can only weep as I have to tell you that Niccolò, our father, died here on this 22nd, of stomach pains caused by a medicine he took on the 20th. He allowed Brother Matteo, who was with him to the last, to hear his confession. Our father, as you know, left us in direst poverty. When you come back this way I shall have a great deal to tell you. Just now I am in a great hurry and will say no more. My best compliments.

Your Relative,

PIERO MACHIAVELLI.

CASSELL'S
POCKET LIBRARY

An admirable series of good books, printed on thin opaque paper, $7 \times 4\frac{5}{8}$ ins. Cloth, 5s. net.

CASSELL'S
POCKET LIBRARY